SAGE was founded in 1965 by Sara Miller McCune to support the dissemination of usable knowledge by publishing innovative and high-quality research and teaching content. Today, we publish over 900 journals, including those of more than 400 learned societies, more than 800 new books per year, and a growing range of library products including archives, data, case studies, reports, and video. SAGE remains majority-owned by our founder, and after Sara's lifetime will become owned by a charitable trust that secures our continued independence.

Los Angeles | London | New Delhi | Singapore | Washington DC | Melbourne

ADVANCE PRAISE

"An old adage of public relations tells us that there are two rules of crisis communications: (1) communicate early; (2) communicate often. Venke Sharma and Hushidar Kharas's book *The Indestructible Brand* shares keen insights and engaging case studies on the transformation of crisis communications in the 'age of social', and how social media monitoring and engagement can help you prevent, mitigate, and manage your brand in today's complicated marketplace."

—Adam Brown
Executive Strategist, Salesforce.com, USA

"In life, and in business, reputation is everything. That said, reputation is very fragile and it only takes one mistake to cause irreparable damage to your company's image. Venke is a true digital leader with over 17 years' experience in marketing and creating digital experiences for companies. He is an expert in leading a business into the always-on digital media and nurturing brand experiences through the use of strategic social media conversations.

This book is a practical and useful resource for executives looking to develop company and brand transparency and deliver high customer involvement. Ignoring strong public digital voices isn't an option anymore. Companies have to not only communicate effectively in the social media age but truly listen to the social chatter and respond in the way that align with both brand and customer expectations.

The book looks at best practices for integrating social media into your crisis communications strategy, and focuses on how to leverage social media tools and develop company-wide processes to manage and mitigate harmful events that could have long-term consequences for the health of companies and their brands."

—**Adam Good**
Chief Digital Officer, Asia Pacific
Dentsu Inc., Singapore

"Don't be fooled by the title of this book; there is no such thing as an indestructible brand.

Years, even decades, of great service to your constituencies may be undone by just one thoughtless tweet or a mere hour's delay in responding to an untoward event involving your brand. Every brand is now on notice, since mass communication tools are freely available to its dissatisfied consumers, disgruntled employees, and the inevitable ambulance chasers.

As a caring brand custodian, what you can do to pad up for this new world is craft an elaborate policy framework for social listening and response, equip the brand with the right team, train them well, and pray.

Or you could buy many copies of this truly helpful book, and just follow the instructions. The authors have made crisis management feel as easy as putting together an Ikea stool. This book is really a practical, no-nonsense playbook for crisis management that no brand should go without. Seriously, get the book, and act on it."

—Karthi Marshan
Senior Executive Vice President and Head–Marketing
Kotak Mahindra Group, India

"This book is essential reading for any brand that has customers with access to the internet, that is, any brand on the planet. Being a 'brand in the time of social' is tough, and often you're just one customer tweet away from a crisis. From your product to your brand ambassadors to rogue social media accounts, a lot can go wrong and has—as the many brands mentioned in this book will agree. Brands, big and small, need to be prepared and do a lot of scenario planning with a crisis playbook in place and be ready to execute. This book is a doer's handbook loaded with sobering examples and practical how-to's on building your brand's unique crisis playbook and executing to it so you're prepared for the worst—a key step toward building an indestructible brand in the time of social."

—Lakshmanan (Lux) Narayan
Chief Executive Officer and Cofounder,
Unmetric, USA

"We live in a connected era where people are more informed, less loyal, and more demanding. We also live in the age of fake news and low-level divas often screaming for attention. Whilst the best offence is a good defense, prevention is often impossible. With *The Indestructible Brand: Crisis Management in the Age of Social Media*, Venke and Hushi offer practical advice on how companies should expect, react, and manage a social crisis. Do this today to safeguard your hard-earned shares, profits, and reputation."

—Suresh Ramaswamy
Digital Lead and Regional Director, South East Asia
Grey Group, Singapore

"In this age of social media, even the smallest of issues can erupt into a crisis, and it often does. Especially in a country like ours, where the internet is all-pervasive, and netizens want to share everything they read. In this scenario, being crisis-ready is extremely crucial. This book is a brilliant and crisp hands-on guide on how to build a crisis-ready organization. The authors' keen perception and in-depth research is visible in each and every page of the book, and will leave a lasting impact on not only those who head organizations but also on policy-makers. I hope it is also read by the general public, so they get a view of what it takes to control the damage caused by senseless sharing of unverified information."

—Sanjay Tripathy
Senior Executive Vice President
Head–Marketing, Analytics, Digital, and E-Commerce
HDFC Life, India

"'Age of social media' has given a completely new meaning to 'crisis management'—and there is a lack of well-researched content on this topic. I am delighted to see this come from Venke [and Hushi]—most timely and thoughtful. It will be most useful for all marketers."

—Rajesh Kumar Jindal
Vice President, Audience and Experiential Marketing
Asia Pacific and Japan, SAP

"Winning on social is a must for all brands in our connected age. And success means listening with empathy, storytelling with personality, and interacting with respect. But it also means being prepared for the unforeseen and the unpredictable. This book thoroughly depicts the kinds of crises modern companies may face in our fast-moving culture and suggests practical ways to prepare for and handle such situations. This book is a must-read for marketing professionals, brand managers, and indeed all leaders who seek to crisis-proof their brands."

—Rishi Jaitly
Chief Executive Officer, Times Global
Bennett Coleman and Co. Ltd

The Indestructible Brand

The Indestructible Brand

Crisis Management In the Age of Social Media

Venke Sharma
Hushidar Kharas

Los Angeles | London | New Delhi
Singapore | Washington DC | Melbourne

First published in 2017 by

SAGE Publications India Pvt Ltd
B1/I-1 Mohan Cooperative Industrial Area
Mathura Road, New Delhi 110 044, India
www.sagepub.in

SAGE Publications Inc
2455 Teller Road
Thousand Oaks, California 91320, USA

SAGE Publications Ltd
1 Oliver's Yard, 55 City Road
London EC1Y 1SP, United Kingdom

SAGE Publications Asia-Pacific Pte Ltd
3 Church Street
#10-04 Samsung Hub
Singapore 049483

Published by Vivek Mehra for SAGE Publications India Pvt Ltd, typeset in 10.5/15 pt ITC Century Book by Diligent Typesetter India Pvt Ltd, Delhi, and printed at Saurabh Printers Pvt Ltd, Greater Noida.

Library of Congress Cataloging-in-Publication Data Available

ISBN: 978-93-864-4679-4 (PB)

SAGE Team: Manisha Mathews, Sandhya Gola and Rajinder Kaur

We'd like to dedicate this book to everything that makes social media as interesting and fascinating as it is today, the trolls who keep us all on our toes, the fangirls and fanboys without whom no brand could survive, and the overworked and underpaid social media interns whose occasional errors provided us rich material.

Bulk Sales

SAGE India offers special discounts
for purchase of books in bulk.
We also make available special imprints
and excerpts from our books on demand.

For orders and enquiries, write to us at

Marketing Department
SAGE Publications India Pvt Ltd
B1/I-1, Mohan Cooperative Industrial Area
Mathura Road, Post Bag 7
New Delhi 110044, India

E-mail us at **marketing@sagepub.in**

Get to know more about SAGE

Be invited to SAGE events, get on our mailing list.
Write today to **marketing@sagepub.in**

This book is also available as an e-book.

CONTENTS

LIST OF ABBREVIATIONS

CCO	consumer commitment officer
CDC	Center for Disease Control and Prevention
CDO	chief digital officer
CEO	chief executive officer
CFO	chief financial officer
CMO	chief marketing officer
COO	chief operating officer
CRM	customer relationship management
CXO	chief of respective function
ERP	enterprise resource planning
FDA	Food and Drug Authority
FSSAI	Food Safety and Standards Authority of India
HR	human resources
LGBT	lesbian, gay, bisexual, and transgender
ME	Middle East
NGO	nongovernmental organization
PR	public relations
R&D	research and development
SUV	sports utility vehicle
TRAI	Telecom Regulatory Authority of India

FOREWORD

A sane method to the madness of crisis is the best way to describe this book.

In this era of social media, brands are constantly being tried in the court of public opinion, and this creates a need for a well-oiled crisis machine to prevent loss of reputation, revenue, and brand love.

What I loved the most about the book is the concept of a "consumer commitment officer" whose job would be to check if the organization is fulfilling its promise to consumers 24×7.

It sums up what I believe is a truly consumer-centric approach for organizations in the social age; listening to consumers and acting upon their feedback in a timely fashion is the first step in being crisis-ready.

With invaluable lessons from brands that have been caught unaware in the middle of crises, the chapters guide you through a feasible preparatory process for being crisis-ready.

Sanjay Behl
Chief Executive Officer
Raymond Limited, India

PREFACE

We live in a social age, and whether or not your brand is on social media, your consumers are. They are continuously sharing their good and bad experiences about your brand or service. While every brand would love consumers saying good things about them, most brands are not prepared to deal with negative feedback. If ignored, that can soon spiral into a crisis.

This book seeks to aid brand and business owners in structuring organizations to be crisis-ready. We discuss the creation of a crisis squad and a crisis playbook, envisioning various scenarios that can occur and what the brand's response should be. We recommend preventive measures that can save brands from social embarrassment, and social listening strategies that can alert organizations to a problem before it becomes a crisis. When all else fails and a crisis is at hand, the focus shifts to executing the playbook, turning the conversation around leveraging evangelists and influencers. Once the crisis has ended, it's time to audit the playbook and close the gaps, as well as evaluate financial or reputational damage done to the brand and quickly recover.

The objective of this book is to help brand owners evaluate their organization's crisis readiness, take measures to prevent crises where possible, build a crisis plan to respond when the inevitable happens, leverage technology to gain actionable insights in time, every time, and finally master the craft of storytelling to turn the conversation in their favor. We hope that you learn from the several examples highlighted in this book and develop a crisis-ready organization by using the tools mentioned here.

Disclaimer: The views expressed in the book are the authors' own and do not reflect those of the organizations that the authors are currently associated with.

Venke Sharma
Hushidar Kharas

Chapter-1

THE AGE OF CRISIS

In September 2003, a consumer found worms in a bar of Cadbury chocolate in Akurdi, Pune, India. A week later, the same thing happened in Mumbai, and the consumer complained to the Maharashtra Food and Drug Authority (FDA) commissioner. On October 2, the chief chemist at the State Food Laboratory declared that the chocolates were insect infested and unfit for eating. This was followed by the discovery of insect/fungus-infected chocolates in Nagpur and Bangalore in the next 30 days.

The news media picked up the story on October 3, and over the next two months, the story appeared in about 1,000 news clips and 120 TV news mentions. Cadbury's initial response was poor; it claimed that its manufacturing process was infallible and blamed the retailer for improper storage. The FDA countered by stating that airtight packaging was also the company's responsibility. Realizing that the issue was spiraling into a discussion about irresponsible MNCs, the company got its act together. It launched new, dual-layered packaging including a metallic polyflow cover. It also launched "Vishwas" (trust), a retailer education program covering 190,000 points of sale in key states.

At the same time, its public relations (PR) team went into war mode, ensuring that every news article about the issue contained a quote from the brand about what it was doing to solve the problem. Three months later, it launched an ad campaign featuring Bollywood celebrity Amitabh Bachchan, addressing the issue head on by highlighting the new packaging and reassuring consumers. While the company did experience a 4% drop in market share and a 37% decline in net profit for the year, it regained its dominant 70% market share six months after the incident.

In December 2013, Justine Sacco, the communications director of InterActive Corp., made a tasteless Twitter joke linking AIDS and race, before getting on a flight from London to her family home in South Africa. The tweet— "Going to Africa. Hope I don't get AIDS. Just kidding. I'm white!"—was an attempt at humor, albeit about an extremely sensitive subject, especially in the land of her birth. When she landed 11 hours later, she was the number one Twitter trend in the world, with 10,000+ tweets in a matter of hours. The tweet had gone viral on Twitter and BuzzFeed, and her company was in damage-control mode in the middle of the holiday season. InterActive responded quickly, first by communicating that the employee was mid-air and therefore unreachable and then by taking the action of firing her as soon as she landed. The company went largely unscathed, but it took Justine two years to get her life back together.

Going to Africa. Hope I don't get AIDS. Just kidding. I'm white!

On May 20, 2015, the Food Safety and Standards Authority of India (FSSAI) ordered Nestle India to recall Maggi noodles after tests at the Central Food Laboratory in Kolkata, India, showed a higher than permissible amount of lead. The company refuted the charge and initially stated that the packets which had been tested were over a year old and had been kept open for a long time, making them invalid for testing. Over the next 48 hours, the ban was discussed 15,000 times on social media by concerned consumers and pranksters alike; 2-minute jokes abounded. The company responded using its official Twitter handle on May 21, stating that no recall had been ordered, with a link to a press release that refuted the recall. The release also stated that the company was "aware of reports about elevated lead levels" but did not refute these reports. It merely stated that the company regularly monitored for lead as part of its stringent quality control processes.

Over the next 10 days, there were 20,000 more mentions of the issue, with no additional information offered by the brand. On June 1, the brand began to reply to individual consumer queries, starting with Bollywood actress Madhuri Dixit, sharing data from new tests that showed that Maggi was safe. It also replied to and re-tweeted statements from consumers supporting the brand but refrained from taking the issue head on and refuting the lead-level findings.

Eventually, on June 4, 2015, the company was forced to execute a country-wide recall, citing unfounded reports and reiterating that the product was safe for everyone. On June 16, it proceeded to destroy 30,000 tonnes of Maggi, again stating that it put its consumer's interests first and it wanted to eliminate any shadow of a doubt. During this time, there were additional 150,000 social mentions of the crisis. The company put out a continuous flow of information on its website and social media handles and continued to respond to consumers. By early July, it was evident that there was nothing wrong with the product. Food authorities in Britain, Canada, and Singapore, as well as state labs in Karnataka had certified that Maggi was safe. On August 13, the Bombay High Court lifted the ban on Maggi, and by November, it was back on the shelves. At a financial level, Maggi's market share declined from 77% in January 2015 to 44% in January 2016, and Nestle India's stock price went down from ₹7,000 on May 19, 2015, to ₹5,500 on June 8, 2015. As of April 24, 2017, the share price was hovering at ₹6305.

Nestle's response to the crisis did not differ significantly from Cadbury's. It refuted the charges, took relatively quick action on the ground, and communicated regularly with the consumer (except for the 10-day gap between May 21 and June 1). The one major thing it could have done differently was to take the issue head on, instead of saying things like "we're aware of reports" or "we are yet to receive official notice." The results, however, were dramatically different. Nestle suffered much larger financial losses, and the incident allowed competitors to capture precious market share. More importantly, it allowed a trust deficit to develop amidst the consumers of a cult brand, when there was nothing really wrong with the product. The difference between the two was created by the phenomenon that we call social media. While Nestle was waiting for official communication from government agencies, or results from independent tests, it was being tried in the court of public opinion.

The point we're trying to make is that crises are not a new phenomenon. What has changed is the rate of dispersion and the dynamics between consumer expression, mass media, and government action. Given the current distrust of mass media (especially in India), there is a disproportionate amount of power being vested on social platforms, with very little responsibility. Online news picks up stories from social, and TV news picks up stories from online news. It can all go downhill very quickly, if timely and direct action is not taken.

Varied opinions exist about whether or not this is a good thing for society, but that's beside the point. Whether we like it or not, social is here to stay; it can have tremendous impact on critical business metrics including market share, stock price, and regulatory action. Social media may not be an essential part of your marketing mix, but social listening and crisis preparedness are critical for every organization, whether directly facing consumer or not. Chiefs of respective functions (CXOs), marketers, corporate communication teams, and advertising and PR professionals need to reexamine their ways of working to become crisis-ready.

The Entitlement Generation

We've been hearing for years the adage that the consumer is king, and today's consumers certainly believe that they are. They expect great products and services and are willing to speak out against any real or perceived injustice. They believe that their views matter to companies and expect their concerns to be resolved, usually with a sweetener added on.

A classic example of a frivolous complaint is that of a UK-based law student, Saima Ahmed, who purchased a multipack of Kit Kat candy bars and found the biscuit element missing. She wrote a letter to the chief executive officer (CEO) of Nestle, claiming a loss of emotional and monetary significance and threatening legal action if she wasn't given a lifetime supply of Kit Kat. In this case, internet commenters took the brand's side, calling out the consumer for an "entitlement mindset" and suggesting she accept a refund and let the matter rest.

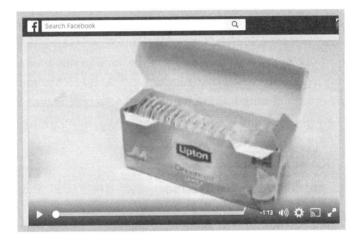

At other times, a consumer may be wrong or may be acting out of ill intent. A video claiming that Lipton Green Tea contained worms went viral in the Middle East (ME). The company's reaction was spot on; it picked it up quickly and replied conclusively with video evidence that the "worms" being shown in the video were simply flavor pieces dissolving into the hot water. It issued responses on the same platforms where the issue had been raised and even created a microsite on its ME page where it hosted the video. It even got local authorities (Food Health Inspection department of the Municipality of Dubai) to visit the facility and put a statement on its own social platforms declaring the tea was safe to drink.

In similar circumstances, Gurugram (previously Gurgaon) resident Neha Tomar took to Facebook to complain about a pack of Amul milk which had turned into a rubbery substance when she tried to make cheese out of it.

The Amul team immediately visited the consumer, evaluated the situation, and put out a response video. They stated that the milk had expired in the consumer's fridge, and the rubbery substance was a natural result of acidifying milk, with a consistency similar to that of mozzarella. They demonstrated this by replicating the process with a fresh batch of milk. They also implied malintent, stating that the consumer had posted on Facebook a day before contacting Amul consumer care and misrepresented the facts of the case.

Neha Tomar added 4 new photos — 😠 feeling mad at 📍 JMD Gardens Sohna Road Gurgaon.
October 10, 2014 · Gurgaon · ✎

Dear all,

This is my personal experience of amul gold milk, which i consume daily. This happened today morning when my mother-in-law took out the milk for our consumption. When she noticed that the milk has got sour she went to the respective vendor from whom we have purchased it, but the vendor refused to take it back. She came back home and thought of making cheese out of the milk and when we started boiling the milk, within 2 min what came out is shown in these pictures. It is some dangerous substance that came out. I thank to god that my family did not consumed this milk. I wonder what would have happened if we would have consumed this. I request everyone to stop taking amul milk, as we need to take strict actions to stop amul from making this deadly milk.

Please spread this message so that respective authorities can take strict, stringent actions against amul.

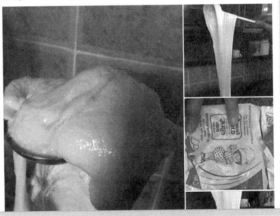

In both these cases, the speedy action taken by the company on ground (visiting the consumer or calling in the health authorities) followed by a clear video response on digital and social led to the incidents being contained effectively. In the long run, this probably enhanced the faith that consumers had in both brands.

Amul added 2 new photos — with Amit Mittal and Suman Bishnoi Mathur.
October 14, 2014 · 🌐

This is regarding the Facebook post that Ms Neha Tomar has shared on her wall. The details of the matter are as follows:

The consumer called our customer care on 10th morning at 9.22 am and shared her experience of using Amul Gold Milk on the very same day. She also emailed the complaint to our official email ID on 10th afternoon. As informed by her, the "use by" date of the Amul Milk was 9th of October. The milk got expired in her fridge which was later used by the consumer.

However, it may be noted that Ms Neha posted her grievance on her Facebook page on 9th October, a day prior to her informing us about the same. Ms Neha Tomar's post on Facebook on 9th Oct, screenshot attached.

Our officials asked the customer that if she has faced the problem on 10th Oct, how is it possible for you to post the same on 9th on Facebook? We now see that the timing of her post has been changed to 10th.

On 11th, we visited her residence in Gurgaon and discussed the above. On 13th we once again visited the customer and provided technical reasons for the incident. We informed her that we checked all the batches of the same Amul Milk and found that there is no problem in any batches including the one which consumer had purchased.

As mentioned in her post, the consumer was trying to make cheese from sour milk which turned out to be a stretchy mass. Let us explain why this happened.

Any natural milk (branded/unbranded) which is acidified (sour) in the chilled condition and then heated shall result in curd mass which shows stretching property similar to that of mozzarella cheese. We have demonstrated the same in the video attached in which we have used fresh milk, acidified to the pH 5.2 and heated to obtain similar mass as shown by the complainant.
Video: http://goo.gl/kOJ74R

We do not understand that why the consumer used her official position to make such complaint without knowing the fact.

On April 9, 2017, United Airlines Flight 3411 from Chicago to Louisville was overbooked. The airline staff tried to offload a few passengers. They used physical force to offload one of the passengers, Dr David Dao, who resisted. At least two passengers posted videos of the physical confrontation and a bleeding Dr Dao's anguished protests; their videos spread rapidly on social media. Sympathy poured for Dr Dao, and United, trending worldwide, found itself in a global crisis of an epic scale.

The next day, United CEO Oscar Munoz issued his first public statement. He acknowledged that a few passengers had to be "re-accommodated." But hours later, a letter sent by him to the airline's employees became public, leading to more hatred for the brand. In the letter, Munoz had lauded the behavior of the flight crew in dealing with a "disruptive and belligerent" passenger. He had credited employees with following established procedures on the Louisville-bound flight. "This situation was unfortunately compounded when one of the passengers we politely asked to deplane refused, and it became necessary to contact Chicago Aviation Security Officers to help," the letter said. "While I deeply regret this situation arose, I also emphatically stand behind all of you, and I want to commend you for continuing to go above and beyond to ensure we fly right."

This apology (or lack thereof) further incensed the public sentiment, with many fliers claiming to cancel their United tickets and vouching to never fly United again. People felt the company and its CEO did not even apologize to the passenger who was manhandled.

The incident catapulted into a storm very quickly, and shares in United Continental Holdings fell on April 11 as the company continued to draw fierce criticism. In mid-morning trading on Wall Street, shares in the group were down around 4%, temporarily wiping close to US$1 billion off the company's total market value.

This forced the CEO to issue a more formal apology: "I continue to be disturbed by what happened on this flight, and I deeply apologize to the customer forcibly removed and to all the customers aboard." The company also retracted its earlier statement and claimed the flight was not overbooked, but the passengers were offloaded to accommodate airline staff who were to operate from Louisville the next day after the mandatory rest.

By then, thousands of tweets, social posts, memes, newspaper articles, and negative television coverage had damaged brand United. The brand did not seem to have a crisis management plan in place, or it didn't execute it if it had one.

Each such crisis is an opportunity to demonstrate how responsive you are to your consumer and how much pride you take in your product/service. Equally, inaction or the perception of inaction can allow a relatively isolated incident to spiral out of control and lead to a huge loss of faith. In the Maggi case, Nestle had a brand with an almost fanatical following. All that consumers needed was a clear rebuttal from the brand, giving them a flag to rally around. When it wasn't forthcoming, they retired to the sidelines, allowing the sentiment to turn against the brand. While Nestle is now vindicated, it will take a long time and much investment before it regains its dominant market share.

References

Cadbury

http://archive.financialexpress.com/news/fda-begins-seizure-of-cadbury-chocolates-after-finding-worms/94351 (accessed on April 11, 2017).

http://timesofindia.indiatimes.com/india/No-worms-in-chocolates-says-Cadbury/articleshow/220596.cms (accessed on April 11, 2017).

http://timesofindia.indiatimes.com/city/mumbai/Some-more-worms-in-Cadbury-chocolate/articleshow/232235.cms (accessed on April 11, 2017).

http://www.hindunet.org/onps/default.php?dtstr=20031005&Formsearchresults_Page=3 (accessed on April 11, 2017).

http://www.business-standard.com/article/companies/cadbury-recovers-from-worm-shock-104070301003_1.html (accessed on April 11, 2017).

http://www.rediff.com/money/2006/dec/24cad.htm (accessed on April 11, 2017).

BP

http://www.theguardian.com/environment/2010/jun/29/bp-oil-spill-timeline-deepwater-horizon (accessed on April 11, 2017).

http://techcrunch.com/2010/06/26/bp-pr-bpglobalpr/ (accessed on April 11, 2017).

http://www.wired.com/2010/06/bps-social-media-campaign-going-about-as-well-as-capping-that-well/ (accessed on April 11, 2017).

http://www.reuters.com/article/us-oil-spill-bp-pr-idUS-TRE65S3JL20100629 (accessed on April 11, 2017).

http://marketrealist.com/2014/09/bp-lost-55-shareholder-value-deep-water-horizon-incident/ (accessed on April 11, 2017).

http://www.nbcnews.com/id/37647218/#.Vujy-eJ97IU (accessed on April 11, 2017).

Justin Sacco

http://www.nytimes.com/2015/02/15/magazine/how-one-stupid-tweet-ruined-justine-saccos-life.html (accessed on April 11, 2017).

Maggi

http://www.hindustantimes.com/columns/lesson-abound-from-nestle-s-maggi-crisis/story-pk6kQlzRV0qbNZ1PfbJ3GK.html (accessed on April 11, 2017).

http://www.business-standard.com/article/news-ians/timeline-of-maggi-noodles-ban-115081300999_1.html (accessed on April 11, 2017).

http://www.hindustantimes.com/columns/lesson-abound-from-nestle-s-maggi-crisis/story-pk6kQlzRV0qbNZ1PfbJ3GK.html (accessed on April 11, 2017).

United Airlines

http://www.independent.co.uk/news/business/news/united-airlines-united-continental-shares-slide-drop-expect-passenger-dragged-flight-3411-overbooked-a7678051.html (accessed on April 13, 2017).

https://www.nytimes.com/2017/04/10/business/united-flight-passenger-dragged.html (accessed on April 13, 2017).

https://www.usatoday.com/story/news/nation/2017/04/11/united-ceo-employees-followed-procedures-flier-belligerent/100317166/ (accessed on April 13, 2017).

Official press release

https://www.nestle.in/media/pressreleases/maggi-noodles-no-recall-msg-lead-confusion (accessed on April 11, 2017).

https://www.nestle.in/media/statements/statement-regarding-ncdrc (accessed on April 11, 2017).

https://www.unileverme.com/news/press-releases/2016/lipton-green-tea-bags-clear-of-any-animate-objects.html (accessed on April 26, 2017).

Tweets

https://twitter.com/MaggiIndia/status/601444189675520000 (accessed on April 11, 2017).

Chapter-2

CREATING A CRISIS-READY ORGANIZATION

> "We don't have a choice on whether we do social media, the question is how well we do it."

> —Erik Qualman

Once you've read through the first chapter, we hope you're convinced that crises are virtually inevitable in the age of social media, which is why it's imperative to get your organization crisis-ready. So how do you get started? The biggest block most organizations face is that crisis management is thought of as a part-time job, to be handled by marketing or corporate communications in their spare time.

"OUR LAST MINUTE PLANS HAVE ALWAYS WORKED. WE NEVER MESSED UP UNTIL NOW."

The absolute first thing you need to do is to hire or appoint a consumer commitment officer (CCO). The CCO heads the crisis squad and owns the crisis playbook. Ideally, he/she should report directly to the CEO or business head and be empowered to reach out and drag the CEO out of a board meeting in case of a serious crisis. While the chief marketing officer (CMO) is responsible for crafting and communicating the brand promise to consumers, it's the CCO's job to check whether the organization is fulfilling that promise 24×7×365. Social listening and customer relationship management (CRM) are two key sources of information that allow him/her to do this. We will not get into a detailed discussion of CRM in this book, but a few aspects that affect crisis prepared-ness and management are crucial and must be mentioned.

Remember that CRM is largely inbound, which means that a consumer is taking a significant effort to reach out to you. This means that only those who are extremely upset or extremely happy with the brand will reach out; you're missing 96%[1] of your consumers who are somewhere in the middle. Clearly, you cannot use this 4% as a sentiment bellwether for the larger consumer base. However, there is a wealth of information hidden in the many brickbats and (usually) fewer bouquets that are lobbed at your email/social/website CRM channel. The first thing to do is tagging them, separating them into positives and negatives, and then attributing them to a specific piece

---

[1] The number is assumed, not validated.

of the business (production, distribution, sales, marketing, and so on).

While the positives are good to know and can be used to recognize teams that are doing a great job, most of the learning will come from the negatives. Draw up trend lines for the negative data on a daily/weekly basis and identify spikes or troughs. Map your business onto this trend line and see how much business-driven seasonality you can eliminate. For example, a price increase for a flagship meal or the discontinuation of a popular beverage will drive a large spike in negative mentions for a few days. If this decision is set in stone, you can tag and then ignore that spike. Identifying spikes that can't be explained is critical to preempting crises.

The marketplace has become extremely consumer-centric, but organizations still have legacy structures and processes that slow them down. Many organizations have systems to track and resolve complaints, but too often the complaint is "closed" rather than truly resolved, and it just takes one angry consumer to start a crisis, especially if other consumers have hitherto been suffering in silence and choose to jump on the bandwagon.

Organizations that have a direct consumer interface like a retail or restaurant chain should keep an eagle eye on service complaints. These should be resolved at the retail level in a maximum of 24 hours, with a recorded communication from the restaurant/store manager that the consumer is no longer irate and has accepted the apology from the restaurant or that he is satisfied with the corrective action taken by the restaurant. If not closed in 24 hours, the CCO must be alerted and must track the issue on a daily basis until closed. It's important that the root cause of the issue is identified and fixed, so the issue does not recur.

WE ARE
CRISIS-READY
24 X 7 AND
DOUBLY SO ON
WEEKENDS!
TRY US!

The second crucial asset the CCO has is social listening, which is so critical to crisis management that we've devoted an entire chapter to it (see Chapter 5). We will dwell in detail on how to set it up and execute it. Here is why it is important though—while your CRM initiatives may pick up specific mentions of the brand page or handle, social listening allows you to track any mention of your brand, product, campaigns, leadership, or anything related to your business. Most importantly, it reduces information asymmetry by ensuring that you know at least as much as your consumer does about an incident that could become a crisis.

Social listening is an excellent way to gather information on a lot more of that missing 96%, as it captures what consumers are saying about your brand and business without being prompted or incentivized. Reading net sentiment is a fair indicator of how your consumers perceive your brand. While machine-generated sentiment has its flaws, it can be taught and it becomes a strong indicator with sufficient data volumes. Again, tagging each mention is critical whether done via automation or human intervention. Viewing the tagged data on a time axis reveals crucial information about when your consumers choose to talk about you and when they speak most passionately about your brand. Once again, a spike in negative mentions is the precursor to a crisis and should be escalated to the CCO and monitored daily.

Once he/she has his/her social listening and CRM set up, the CCO becomes the eyes and ears of the organization. He/she will be the first to know about anything that may damage the brand and must decide whether an issue can be handled through normal channels or whether it constitutes a crisis. This call can be calibrated by setting volume benchmarks for sensitive keywords; we've discussed this piece in detail in the next chapter "The Crisis Playbook."

Now that you've appointed a CCO, crises are his/her problem, right? Wrong. Crises can occur in any aspect of the business, and it takes a cross-functional team to handle them.

A crisis squad absolutely must contain representation from the PR, product, legal, operations, sales, human resources (HR), and marketing teams. Representation from cross-functional teams is especially critical in larger and more complex organizations. The crisis squad members need not be functional heads, but they should be senior resources who understand the business well and can pull in their functional heads when required. The first thing the CCO does when crisis hits is to reach out to the relevant representative to verify the information that is being shared in the public domain.

Social media and PR go hand in hand, as TV news channels and newspapers routinely pick up stories from happenings on social media. In the case of a crisis, the PR representative on the squad must be kept fully looped in and must prepare to receive questions and calls from journalists who're keen to get a company statement on the crisis. It's critical for the company to get a statement out immediately, even if it's just an initial holding statement. Further details should be released proactively as decisions are implemented. Starting out a crisis with "no comment" only means that you will be left out of the conversation and will make it much harder to reenter the discourse once you've taken an action and are ready to talk about it.

The product and operations representatives are needed if the crisis has occurred at the product/service level. They are best placed to explain the extent of the problem, the circumstances under which it occurred, and the steps being taken to address the problem. The research and development (R&D) or product head can also be a credible spokesperson for the company, once they have been media-trained.

Depending on the nature of the crisis, the CCO may also consult the legal rep to ascertain the regulatory and statutory aspects of the case. Unfortunately, legal teams tend to err on the side of caution and may counsel a wait-and-watch approach. This is almost never a good idea; waiting and watching is often perceived as arrogance and inaction by consumers and only makes things worse. Sensitizing legal reps to the importance of proactive, non-"corporatish" communication is essential to a positive outcome.

The HR rep on the squad has two key roles to play. The first is to ensure that every employee is trained on the employee section of the crisis playbook, which informs them on how to use or not to use their personal social handles in times of crisis. The second is to cascade information to employees during times of crisis so they don't feel like they're the last to know. This is critical to keep morale up and make sure everyone's working to solve the problem at hand.

The brand/marketing rep on the squad owns the story. Crafting communications during a crisis is never easy, with myriad restrictions being enforced by legal or compliance teams. It is important to remember that the message is being created for the consumer, who does not care about compliance and just wants a straight answer. It is critical to get the organization's point of view out, either through direct statements or external endorsements. It is also important to ensure that the brand voice is maintained through a crisis and the brand does not lose its personality under pressure.

Having the CEO involved is a double-edged sword. An engaged CEO is great in times of crisis; consumers know him/her and will listen to his/her point of view. However, if the CEO becomes the default face of the organization, consumers may start writing to him/her directly, bypassing the CRM team. Consumers are realizing that an escalation to the CEO is the best way to get the organization moving. While consumers love such CEOs, when this becomes a pattern it makes the organization's crisis management function CEO-centric. Emails/tweets to the CEO get a disproportionate amount of attention irrespective of their merit and may skew your crisis benchmarks or cause other more important consumer communications to be dealt with less urgently.

Now that we've identified the necessary stakeholders, the next step is to get them crisis-ready. Over the next few chapters, we'll look at creating a crisis playbook, setting up social listening to give the organization an early warning system, and managing assets to minimize the chances of a crisis.

In an ideal scenario, the only thing you should have to do when a crisis hits is execute—all the thinking should have been done beforehand!

The Crisis Squad

Chapter-3

BUILDING A CRISIS PLAYBOOK

"The Chinese use two brush strokes to write the word 'crisis'. One brush stroke stands for danger; the other for opportunity. In a crisis, be aware of the danger—but recognize the opportunity."

—John F. Kennedy

So the crisis squad has been created, and the CCO knows who to call when things go awry. The next step is to huddle and put together the crisis playbook, a concise yet comprehensive list of steps to be taken when a crisis hits. This is ideally done via a workshop where the stakeholders can disconnect from the day-to-day activity and focus on the task at hand.

It is important that all stakeholders are open about the risks that arise in their piece of the business and are not defensive. There's no place for turf wars in the crisis squad, and "this is my problem and I will handle it" is not an acceptable approach. It's up to the CCO to drive the spirit of cooperation, perhaps through a series of teamwork exercises at the start of the session or by role plays that encourage people to think in detail about functions they are otherwise unfamiliar with. Getting an external facilitator for the session is also an option, as it allows reps to talk to a neutral body that sees issues from everyone's perspective.

Possible exercises to get everyone thinking collaboratively are as follows:

1. Ask an R&D person to visualize managing the HR aspect of a crisis.
2. Ask a PR person to identify places in the production, packaging, and distribution processes where a crisis may occur.
3. Play a game where half the squad represents the environment (consumers, competition, partners, and government) and tries to cause crises for the brand, while the other half manages the fort and defends the brands reputation against the assault. The CCO or external facilitator can extend the game until the first team runs out of ideas or call an end when one team is clearly dominating.

We have divided the playbook process into three steps:

Scenario Building: Identifying scenarios from which a crisis can arise for your brand.
Establishing Benchmarks: Setting up qualitative and quantitative benchmarks that differentiate between an issue and crisis and trigger subsequent predefined actions.
The Playbook: A detailed set of instructions and resources for the crisis squad (and for all employees) to be used once the benchmarks have been reached.

Scenario Building

The first step toward creating a crisis playbook is scenario building. Think of everything that can go wrong for your brand/organization. Evaluate issues and crises that may have happened in the past to your organization or competition, or in your business environment. Run through every aspect of your value chain step by step, identifying vulnerabilities. It's important to think like a consumer—make a list of the known negatives and the keywords that consumers tend to use while talking about them. Use the grid below, but feel free to fill in examples that are more relevant to your category.

Product

Your product is your single largest consumer touchpoint and hence has the highest likelihood to set off a crisis. They are also the largest impact crises, affecting consumer perception, financials, and possibly even government relations. When Volkswagen hit #dieselgate, the immediate impact was judicial, the possibility of large judicial penalties and forced recalls. Twelve months later, what we've seen is a huge deterioration in consumer perception and a valuation that's still 20% lower than before the scandal hit. The total financial impact of fines alone is over US$21 billion, and the arrests continue, with 13 senior executives being indicted and the governments of 20 countries still investigating the issue.

Similarly, when Nestle faced product safety issues with Maggi in India, the immediate impact was regulatory—with the FSSAI insisting on a national recall, and tonnes of the product having to be destroyed. There was also a large short-term impact, with market share falling and the market cap of Nestle India dropping 33%. However, the strength of the brand and the cult status it had with customers allowed it to minimize the perception impact, and it bounced back strongly to regain market leadership.

Service

If you operate in a service industry, where you own the last mile touchpoint with consumers, service becomes the next most crisis-prone area, especially when dealing with health threatening categories like food or pharma. The restaurant business is especially crisis-prone, with examples mentioned earlier like the Dominos employees mistreating food in Conover, North Carolina. Another example of employee-driven crisis is KFC, where employees of a KFC in Andersen, California, posted images of themselves bathing in a sink meant for washing dishes on Myspace. While the errant employees were dismissed in both the cases, the damage to the brand is not so easily undone. Burger King has had its share of trouble, with a photo of an employee in Mayfield, Ohio, standing on two bins of lettuce with his boots on! They have had a sink bathing incident as well, when an employee calling himself Mr Unstable posted an image of himself in a

BK sink on 4chan. Taco Bell is not to be left behind, having fired employees for posting images of pretending to urinate on a place of Nachos, or licking a stack of tacos.

Packing and Distribution

While packaging and distribution rarely gets much consumer attention, it can drive severe negative reactions when things go wrong. The best example of this is the Cadbury's incident referenced in Chapter 1, where packaging failures led to multiple instances of worms inside packed chocolate bars.

Regulatory

It is not always something that your organization, employees, or even partners do that creates a crisis. Changes in regulatory guidelines, often caused by completely extraneous factors, can negatively impact your brand and business. For example, the recent ban on diesel vehicles with 2 liter engines in Delhi was driven by smog, which is more a consequence of farmers burning crop stubble and truckers driving 30-year-old machines on low quality fuel than of the small percentage of high displacement sports utility vehicles (SUVs). The impact was significant, however, with Toyota losing business worth ₹17 billion (equivalent to US$263 million) and calling the decision a "Death Sentence" for the industry.

Interestingly, Mahindra was able to react faster, launching a 1990cc version of its signature mHawk engine for its SUVs in the capital, priced the same as its predecessors. Toyota took longer to respond and introduced high displacement petrol engines, which would not appeal as much to the consumer segment.

Similarly, Facebook India walked into a crisis that was almost unrelated to its core business with the "Free Basics" campaign that fell afoul of the Net Neutrality advocates in India. While Facebook's likely intent was to expand its user base in India by subsidizing the internet for its customers, the consumer- and influencer-led campaign to abolish differential access was heard by the Telecom Regulatory Authority of India (TRAI) and resulted in a ruling against Facebook and the telecom companies. Facebook invested a significant amount of its reputational capital as well as marketing budgets behind the campaign, including FaceTime from Mark Zuckerberg, and the failure to secure a positive decision from TRAI was a significant reverse.

Retail

Retail templates are usually standardized across the world with good reason. DKNY, however, ran into a unique issue when its store in Bangkok used images that had been sent to it as "thought starters" as actual store designs. The trouble was that DKNY had negotiated with the photographer (Brandon Stanton of "Humans of New York" fame) and had failed to close on a price. Stanton's fans sent him pictures of the store in Bangkok, and he posted it on his Facebook page asking DKNY to donate US$100,000 to the local Young Men's Christian Association (YMCA). DKNY apologized, explained the miscommunication, and donated US$25,000 to the charity as a settlement.

CRM

CRM is usually the recipient of the effects of a crisis, but in some cases it can cause embarrassment to an organization. In the case of Vodafone India, a smart customer on Twitter noticed that the companies CRM handle was tweeting out standard copy irrespective of the nature of the customer query. He promptly tweeted that he wanted to marry the CEO's daughter and asked for a response by the end of the day. Sure enough, Vodafone customer care responded by asking him for his number and promising to help!

Supply Chain

The upstream supply chain is also a key source of crises. It is not enough to be compliant yourself; you have to ensure that your suppliers are compliant and eco-friendly as well. Apple Inc.'s troubles with its suppliers in China are well documented, with frequent allegations of exploitative labor practices. Similarly, the fast-food industry has been targeted due to its high consumption of palm oil, which is leading to deforestation in Malaysia. KFC Indonesia was targeted for its consumption of paper packaging, largely supplied by Asia Pulp & Paper, a company which has been repeatedly accused by nongovernmental organizations (NGOs) of illegal deforestation in Indonesia leading to the near extinction of native species including the Sumatran tiger.

Marketing

Poorly thought-through marketing campaigns are often the cause of social media crises. In 2012, McDonald's launched a campaign to get people to share their heart-warming Happy Meal experiences with #McDStories. Instead, customers hijacked the hashtag and turned it into a nightmare for the marketing team. Customers shared bad food experiences (food poisoning, poor quality) or brand shaming trivia and jokes. #McDStories was a paid Twitter trend. Seeing the negative buzz, the company reacted promptly and brought down the campaign within two hours. The tweets didn't stop though, as the Twitteratti were on fire. Each story and joke inspired a few more. What's worse, ex-employees joined the bandwagon, talking about the things they had seen in the kitchens that would turn customers away from the brand.

Clearly, McDonald's still had hope in the internet. In 2016, McDonald's New Zealand launched a campaign to get people to create and name their own burger on their website. Older and wiser, they created a profanity filter to weed out abusive texts, but they weren't counting on the ingenuity and creativity of the idle internet user. Pranksters had a field day demonstrating their creativity with political memes and obscene jokes. The web page had to be pulled down hours later.

Public Relations

Guido Barilla, chairman of the world's leading pasta maker Barilla invited rage from netizens when he remarked that he would never use a gay family in Barilla's advertising. He said "I would never do (a commercial) with a homosexual family, not for lack of respect but because we don't agree with them. Ours is a classic family where the woman plays a fundamental role." His comment was in response to a direct question about whether he would ever feature a gay family in his company's commercials. He went on to say, "If gays like our pasta and our advertising, they'll eat our pasta. If they don't like it, then they will not eat it, and they will eat another brand."

As expected, lesbian, gay, bisexual, and transgender (LGBT) rights activists called out a boycott of Barilla pasta. There was a wave of anti-Barilla sentiment across media. Barilla apologized the next day, and the company backed this with a series of measures including making Barilla a very inclusive workspace for the LGBT community. This rapid response ensured a positive response from members of the LGBT community, and the company was able to avoid any adverse impact on its brand and business.

Brand Social Media

In September 2012, Volkswagen launched Polo with a national print campaign in India. It surprised newspaper readers with a motorized device attached on the back page that vibrated automatically when the paper was opened. The vibrations meant to excite readers (giving them the shivers) and make them curious enough to walk into a Volkswagen showroom for a test drive. The campaign received mixed reactions on Twitter, with some users calling it a vibrator. In response, the official Volkswagen India handle tweeted back:

> Women would be dumb to call it a vibrator. Or maybe they do not understand real driving experience. #PunIntended #Volkswagen #Creative

This crass sexist response over the tweet earned the ire of the Twitterverse. Volkswagen promptly deleted the tweet, but several users had taken screenshots of it and the brand continued to receive flak. Volkswagen did not respond for almost three days, and when they did it was the clichéd and patently false explanation that their handle had been compromised.

Brand Ambassador

In November 2015, Bollywood celebrity Aamir Khan created a stir during a journalism award function by saying that his wife Kiran Rao had wondered whether they should move out of the country due to the phenomenon of rising intolerance against minorities.

Khan faced social media outrage for being an anti-national and his name trended on Twitter with abuse primarily originating from right-wing supporters. The Twitteratti broadened their focus to include brands he endorsed and picked Snapdeal, an e-commerce market place, as a good target. Tweets asking users to uninstall Snapdeal from the phone poured in. This was followed with screenshots of actual uninstalls and 1-star ratings of the app on the Google play store being shared on social media.

Rita
@RitaG74

👤 Follow ⌄

#NoToSnapDeal #appwapsi I have uninstalled @snapdeal app from my phone and given them a 1-star Google Playstore review. Remove Amir.

Snapdeal disassociated itself from Khan's remarks, releasing a press statement stating that

> Snapdeal is neither connected nor plays a role in comments made by Aamir Khan in his personal capacity. Snapdeal is a proud Indian company built by passionate young Indians focused on building an inclusive digital India. Every day we are positively impacting thousands of small businesses and millions of consumers in India. We will continue towards our mission of creating one million successful online entrepreneurs in India.

The company subsequently did not renew Khan's contract.

The following table provides a summary of crises which originated from various business functions that can aid one in scenario building:

Origin	Impact	Example
Product	Financial Consumer Government	VW—Diesel engines that cheat emissions tests GM—Ignition switches that catch fire Nestle India—Alleged lead contamination in Maggi

Origin	Impact	Example
Service	Financial Consumer Government	Dominos—Employees mistreating food in Conover, North Carolina KFC—Employees bathing in a sink
Packaging and Distribution	Financial Consumer Government	Cadbury India—Worms in the chocolate
Regulatory Environment	Financial Consumer Government	Toyota and Mahindra—Diesel SUV ban in New Delhi Facebook—Net Neutrality in India TRAI—Telecom companies fined for call drops
Retail	Financial Consumer	DKNY—Bangkok store used Humans of New York photos without licensing them
CRM	Financial Consumer	Vodafone—Template response to request to marry owner's daughter Boingo sends an incorrect "test" email to many of its customers, telling them their subscription plan has changed
Supply Chain	Financial Consumer	Many restaurant chains have faced protests from NGOs like Greenpeace about the deforestation caused by the palm oil used in fryers and the paper used in food packaging
Marketing	Consumer	McDonald's—#McDstories backfired
PR	Financial Consumer	Barilla Pasta CEO makes an anti-gay statement to a set of journalists
Brand Social Media	Consumer	Volkswagen India—"Women don't understand the real driving experience" KitchenAid—Inappropriate tweet about Obama's grandmother

(Continued)

(Continued)

Origin	Impact	Example
Employee Social Media	Consumer	Justine Sacco's tweet caused her employer to be put under a spotlight
Brand Ambassador	Financial Consumer	Aamir Khan's controversy drove Snapdeal app uninstalls

Establishing Benchmarks

The next step is to set qualitative and quantitative benchmarks to distinguish between a consumer issue and a full-blown crisis. A degree of judgment will need to be exercised as well, but having numerical benchmarks makes it a lot easier to filter and avoid false alarms.

These will vary drastically for different types of crises, for example, 1 negative mention about a product hygiene issue (spitting in a pizza) is enough to go into crisis mode, but it may take 50 or 100 mentions/hour of a known negative (network outage for a telecom or flight delays for an airline) to initiate action. Benchmarks need to be time-bound; velocity is a key component of a social crisis; things that pick up speed quickly are likely to blow out of proportion. It's also important to see where the mentions are coming from. Identify key influencers in your category (celebrity food bloggers), consumer forums, and major news services and create a dashboard dedicated to them.

It is possible to take this a step further and set up successive triggers for a worsening crisis. Each new level of negativity can spur a predefined action such as hiring an ambassador or launching a campaign.

Building the Playbook

So, now you have a clear idea of the various things that can go wrong. What next? How does this help you when a crisis hits? Follow the 10 steps below to put together your crisis playbook. Feel free to add more information that you feel is relevant to your organization or industry, but avoid removing any of the elements shared below:

\#   Start with the basics (Owner: CCO)

- Names, email addresses, and phone numbers for each of the members of the crisis squad and a backup for each of them in case they're unavailable.
- Similar contact details for each of the digital/advertising/PR/CRM agencies.
- Contact details for the person/people with access to the brands social and digital assets (Facebook page, Twitter handle, LinkedIn profile, and website).

\#   Identify the right organizational spokesperson for each kind of crisis (Owner: CCO)

- Ideally, you should have not more than three spokespersons, possibly the CEO, chief financial officer (CFO), and chief operating officer (COO).

Include contact details for each of them and a backup.

- Conduct media training for each of them; focus on body language, dress code, and choice of vocabulary.

- Create a code of conduct for these and other highly visible employees. During a crisis, especially one that impacts consumers or small traders, senior employees should not be seen having fun or displaying conspicuous wealth. Such actions are picked up as signs of arrogance or not caring.

Note: While these may seem obvious, remember that you're being tried in the court of public opinion, where every word and expression will be replayed over and over on TV news. Body language is critical; if you're apologizing, you need to look sorry. Attempts at humor to defuse the situation are unlikely to work. Also, statements are likely to be taken out of context to drum up TRPs and clicks, so be very, very specific with your choice of vocabulary. When the BP Deepwater spill occurred, the CEO Tony Hayward was clearly uncomfortable with all the press attention. His statements such as "We're sorry for the massive disruption it's caused their lives. There's no one who wants this over more than I do. I would like my life back" and "The Gulf of Mexico is a very big ocean. The amount of volume of oil and dispersant we are putting into it is tiny in relation to the total water volume" were taken out of context, and the US news industry went to town showcasing him as a British CEO who didn't care about the damage his company was doing to America.

In another instance, Vijay Mallya of Kingfisher fame was seen celebrating his birthday with calendar models while his airline faced bankruptcy and staff hadn't been paid for months. Actions like that convicted him in the court of public opinion, even as banks and government agencies were starting to close in on him. He's stated several times since then that he feels like he's being made a scapegoat because of his lifestyle, but much of the fault lies with him and his PR team. He did not demonstrate any kind of distress or empathy and has been cast as the villain as a result. Now that he has absconded to the UK, and does not display any intent of returning to India to answer the charges against him, the effect is magnified manifold.

Plan your response strategy (Owner: CCO)

- Are you going to respond to each consumer talking about the crisis, or only those who directly contact the brand?
- Do you need extra hands on deck to handle the increased query volume?
- Can your CRM team/agency handle this? If not, then where can you pull in additional personnel from?

Recommendation

Start with a public, proactive statement addressing the issue, disseminated across multiple platforms. Promote that statement with paid reach; ensure it is easily discoverable.

Next, publicly announce extended customer service timings to show that you want to answer more consumers at times which are more convenient to them. Answer every unique case where consumers are worried about their personal data or their transactional history with the company. Do not, however, try to answer every repetitive queries or complaints where you don't have something different to say to each one of them. Using a template response repetitively makes brands seem like automatons and distances them from the consumer.

Finally, avoid humor unless it's deeply rooted in the brand philosophy and the crisis has no immediate fallout on human life and wellness.

Prepare draft statements for first response (Owner: Marketing/PR)

- These should be preapproved by legal/compliance and can be put out quickly when the crisis is detected.
- Acknowledge that you are aware of the issue, are investigating, and convey a timeline when updates or more details will be shared.
- Use the same medium (Facebook, Twitter, or YouTube) where the crisis first surfaced to issue the response.

Have a preapproved crisis budget and plan how to use it (Owner: Marketing)

- Production costs for digital, print, and TV content as needed, along with a preapproved rate card.
- Media plan to respond on social platforms where the crisis originated.
- Leverage sharp targeted paid media (sponsored stories/tweets or YouTube-promoted videos) to deliver your response to people before or after they view the crisis material. Don't try and stop consumers from seeing it; just ensure that your side of the story is also being told.
- If your organization uses an enterprise resource planning (ERP)-driven payments model, make sure a system allocation exists for this budget. The last thing you want to be doing during a crisis is scrambling for an accounts guy to process paperwork.

\# Pre-align video creation resources within or outside the organization to be ready to produce video response statements. This may be an internal production team or a PR/digital agency (Owner: Marketing)

- Define the turnaround time and rate card for crisis communications.
- Ensure that a Non-Disclosure Agreement (NDA)/ contract is in place with any external partner.

\# Identify independent laboratories, third-party audit agencies, or any other credible external resources that you may need to activate (Owner: R&D/QA/Product)

- Establish terms of engagement where possible (rate cards, NDAs, turnaround times) so that you don't waste time negotiating or making suboptimal decisions.
- Create content seeding and media plans for the output (lab reports, audits, environmental impact assessments) that enable them to reach consumers who have been tracking the crisis.

Identify social influencers or domain experts with a social media presence that you can reach out to at any stage of the crisis management process (Owner: Marketing)

- Identify a showcase facility they can visit (lab, factory, store, or restaurant) where you can demonstrate robust standards and generate a positive impression.

Identify government agencies that are likely to be called in for a crisis in your industry (Owner: Legal/ Compliance)

- Include key personnel and contact details (addresses, phone numbers, websites).

Manage employee communication (Owner: HR)

The crisis playbook needs to have a separate section for employees, telling them how to manage their social interactions during a crisis. The section should be cascaded to all employees as soon as the playbook is ready; don't wait for a crisis to send this out. If an overarching organizational social media policy exists, the crisis section can be integrated into it.

Most employees will have personal profiles and handles and may notice negative mentions about the organization. Their first instinct will be to get into the conversation and defend the company, but that's rarely a good idea. Employees should not be used as mouthpieces during times of crises. At most, if they are directly tagged with questions, they can refer the tagger to the official statement released by the company spokesperson. All official responses should only be issued from the brand handle. It is important to remember that social media conversations are glaringly public and can be used in different contexts for or against the organization.

There is, however, an extremely important function that employees can perform to mitigate or assist during a crisis. Employees will sometimes pick up a negative mention that escapes your social listening practice, either due to privacy restrictions (Facebook) or incomplete query building. They should highlight these at once to the HR representative on the crisis squad. If they don't get a response in two hours, they should escalate to the CCO. It is important that every employee knows that he/she should never hide an issue from leadership; it will eventually explode. Escalate, ring the alarm bells early, and get everyone into war mode as soon as possible.

You Are Now Crisis Ready!

Once all these elements have been put in place, and everyone on the team is fully aligned to their tasks, you are well on your way to being able to manage a crisis. Ensure that the playbook exists in both physical and digital forms and can be accessed from anywhere in the world. Also remember that this data will change on a periodic basis, so make sure the playbook is updated at least once a quarter.

References

VW Dieselgate

http://www.forbes.com/sites/bertelschmitt/2017/01/12/diesel-gate-15-vw-managers-indicted-around-the-world-big-guys-unbothered/#52e9814b7e63 (accessed on April 11, 2017).

Domino's handled social crisis well

http://www.prsa.org/Intelligence/TheStrategist/Articles/view/8226/102/Domino_s_Delivers_During_Crisis_The_Company_s_Step#.VzhV4Pl97IU (accessed on April 11, 2017).

DKNY store in Bangkok uses unlicensed HONY (Humans of New York) photos

http://www.theguardian.com/artanddesign/us-news-blog/2013/feb/25/dkny-pay-photographer-without-permission (accessed on April 11, 2017).

Tony Hayward's statements

http://www.bbc.com/news/10360084 (accessed on April 11, 2017).

Vijay Mallya—Flashy lifestyle despite debt

http://www.ft.com/cms/s/0/85252402-1249-11e6-839f-2922947098f0.html (accessed on April 11, 2017).

Restaurant employees creating crises

http://www.businessinsider.in/Fast-Food-Employees-Keep-Posting-Gross-Photos-Online/articleshow/21310987.cms (accessed on April 11, 2017).

Asia Pulp & Paper—Deforestation

http://www.greenpeace.org/international/en/campaigns/forests/asia-pacific/app/ (accessed on April 11, 2017).

McDonald's

http://www.forbes.com/sites/kashmirhill/2012/01/24/mcdstories-when-a-hashtag-becomes-a-bashtag/#55a0ac91193f (accessed on April 11, 2017).
http://www.telegraph.co.uk/news/2016/07/21/mcdonalds-invites-people-to-create-and-name-their-own-burgers-on/ (accessed on April 11, 2017).

Barilla Pasta

http://www.reuters.com/article/italy-gay-pasta-idUSL5N0HM2O120130926 (accessed on April 11, 2017).
http://www.huffingtonpost.in/entry/barilla-pasta-diversity-initative_n_4212723 (accessed on April 11, 2017).

Volkswagen

http://lighthouseinsights.in/volkswagen-india-twitter-fail-story.html/ (accessed on April 11, 2017).

Aamir Khan—Snapdeal impact

http://www.hindustantimes.com/india/appwapsi-snapdeal-gets-blowback-from-aamir-khan-controversy/story-N3HwOObJ0W-Me9vz7GjXFBO.html (accessed on April 11, 2017).

http://economictimes.indiatimes.com/magazines/panache/snapdeal-releases-official-statement-on-aamir-khan-controversy/article-show/49919825.cms (accessed on April 11, 2017).

SECURING YOUR DIGITAL ASSETS

Digital has clearly established itself as a critical component of any brand's marketing efforts. But what is digital? Digital is less homogenous, more interconnected, and less discrete but more measurable than the emerging media of the past. The lines between social networks, chat, email, and even news have blurred completely, leaving marketers a plethora of continuously evolving platforms to deal with. New platforms offer new avenues to brands for consumer engagement, as well as the opportunity to be "with it" for a while until the competition catches up. This has led to brand managers jumping onto every new trend or fad, perhaps spurred by the fear of missing out. There are three major areas where vulnerabilities can creep in to your digital assets: outdated or expired assets, credentials shared with external agencies, and the lack of capable and mature owners for social handles within organizations.

Virtual Junk

Brands have websites; mobile apps; Facebook pages; Twitter handles; LinkedIn pages; Instagram, Vine, Snapchat, Pinterest accounts; YouTube channels; Google+ pages; and much more. Older assets are forgotten as new technologies take center stage. Remember that awesome app you once had on a Facebook tab? Or that cool campaign microsite that you created in 2012? Or the corporate blog you started but never really found the time to update? Are they still out there? Does anyone have access to them? Would you even know how to take them down, if you wanted to? With frequent changes in priorities and personnel, there's an overwhelming amount of digital assets whose credentials have gone missing. Imagine the internet as a virtual manifestation of space; there's a lot of junk floating around that no one really remembers or thinks about until it crashes into something important!

Agencies

Brands use many external agencies to build and maintain digital assets. They also frequently change these agencies, as people and technology enter and leave the ecosystem. This can lead to assets being lost or compromised, through either carelessness or malicious intent.

In March 2011, the Chrysler official Twitter handle tweeted:

> I find it ironic that Detroic is known as the #motorcity, and yet no one here knows how to f***ing drive.

The Twitterati had a field day with this, not only because Chrysler used the "F" word but also because this message was at odds with Chrysler's "Celebrating Detroit" campaign.

Chrysler responded with an apology, but the damage was done.

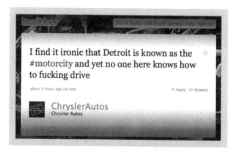

Chrysler Group and its brands do not tolerate inappropriate language or behavior, and apologize to anyone who may have been offended by this communication.

Deleting tweets and apologizing is all very well, but screen-shots survive forever. What happened in this case was that

Chrysler's digital agency, New Media Strategies, had access to its Twitter handle. The agency's executive used the same device to access his personal Twitter account and Chrysler's account. What he meant as an insightful and humorous tweet from his personal handle was accidentally posted on Chrysler's official one, leading to a PR nightmare for Chrysler. This was a failure at multiple levels, with Chrysler not being in full control on what was being posted from its social handle, the agency not following a maker-checker process, and the fact that the same device had access to a personal and a professional social account.

This is hardly a unique case; in September 2012, Volkswagen India published a highly sexist tweet indicating that women do not understand the "real driving experience." Consumers on social media expressed their outrage, the tweet was deleted, and Volkswagen later apologized, stating that their account had been compromised.

In December 2013, the Pepsi India handle tweeted "Supreme Court so gay" in response to a section 370 ruling from the apex court. Predictably, the tweet was deleted and Pepsi stated that its account had been compromised and that it was investigating.

The Right Owners

Brands often delegate social media, especially Twitter (and now Instagram and Snapchat), to the youngest, least experienced, and often lowest paid (or unpaid) trainee or intern on the grounds that "they understand the youth/platform." You don't need us to tell you why that's wrong. Your brand's official Twitter handle is effectively equivalent to your official spokesperson. That's probably your CEO, COO, or CMO. Do you really want that handle being managed by someone who's got a lot to learn about the corporate workplace? The HMV case below is a great example of how wrong this can go!

In January 2013, HMV was in the middle of administration proceedings, when the company's Twitter handle went rogue. The first sign that something was wrong was the tweet "We're tweeting live from HR where we're all being fired! Exciting! #hmvXFactorFiring." Over the next couple of hours, tweets were published about how "mass executions" were underway and the people most loyal to the brand were being sacked. The most interesting tweet, however, was this one—"Just overheard our Marketing Director (he's staying, folks) ask 'How do I shut down Twitter?' #hmvXFactorFiring."

hmv ✔
@hmvtweets
The Official hmv Twitter. The music, film, games and tech you love.
#WeAreEntertainment
UK · http://www.hmv.com

22,489 **981** **62,561** 🐦 Follow
TWEETS FOLLOWING FOLLOWERS

Tweets All / No replies

hmv @hmvtweets   11m
So really, what have we to lose? It's been a pleasure folks! Best
wishes to you all!
Expand

hmv @hmvtweets   14m
Especially since these accounts were set up by an intern (unpaid,
technically illegal) two years ago.
Expand

hmv @hmvtweets   16m
...and those hard working individuals, who wanted to make hmv great
again, have mostly been fired, there seemed no other choice.
Expand

hmv @hmvtweets   17m
Under usual circumstances, we'd never dare do such a thing as this.
However, when the company you dearly love is being ruined...
Expand

It seems the social accounts had been created by an
unpaid intern two years before. The company was now
firing the people with access to the Twitter handle but
had not considered transitioning or changing the social
credentials. If that wasn't bad enough, the one person not
being sacked (the marketing director) did not know how

to access the brand's official handle. Let alone "shutting down Twitter," he would have been unable to even delete the tweets or apologize to consumers without help from the local Twitter office.

So what's this chapter about? Well prevention is, as they say, better than any cure, so we'll look at ways to minimize the risk of a social-media-driven crisis. We'll start with creating an asset inventory, listing down owners of each asset, and restricting credential access to them. We'll then look at technology solutions to drive accountability, enable auditing, and enhance compliance for content that is published on a brand's digital assets. Finally, we'll identify people who can help—agencies to track down counterfeit or copyright content, or contact points at major social platforms who can help you in case your assets do get compromised.

THE COMMANDMENTS

1. THOU SHALT KNOW THY ASSETS
2. THOU SHALT CONTROL THY CREDENTIALS
3. THOU SHALT LEVERAGE TECHNOLOGY
4. THOU SHALT CENTRALISE LOGIN CREDENTIALS
5. THY MAKER ≠ THY CHECKER
6. THOU SHALT NOT MIX BUSINESS AND PLEASURE
7. THOU SHALT VERIFY YOUR ASSETS
8. THOU SHALT SEEK OUT THY ALLIES
9. THOU SHALT SAFEGUARD THY CUSTOMERS' DATA
10. THOU SHALT EDUCATE THY AMBASSADORS

1. Thou Shalt Know Thy Assets

The CCO should create an inventory of "all" social assets, including the agencies that have built them, an owner within the organization, and a protocol for taking them down in a hurry. Any asset that is no longer in use should be unpublished and the data taken offline and stored securely. In case an agency is fired or an employee leaves the organization, create a transition protocol and change passwords to ensure security. The asset inventory should include the following:

a.   Websites: Organizations typically have multiple websites, each with their own stakeholders. There's usually a corporate site, product or ecommerce site, and one or more campaign microsites.

b.   Apps: It's ideal to have just one app that contains the stuff your consumer really wants or finds relevant. However, different functions within a business sometimes create their own apps. Make sure you've got them all!

c.   Social Handles/Pages/Accounts: Social assets are the chief cause of marketing-led crises and should be handled very carefully. While most organizations only use social media to connect with consumers, in some cases, functions like HR may use them to connect with current or potential employees. Ensure that all these assets are included in the inventory, and delete anything that no longer serves a purpose.

2. Thou Shalt Control Thy Credentials

Review the list of internal and external resources who currently have publishing/credentials access and evaluate the need for them to have it. Restrict the number of people who need to know passwords. Others can be given analyst access (for insights) or access to a publishing tool through which they can push out content. Credentials access that is given to external parties (for app or website integration testing) should be specific to a closely monitored time frame.

In February 2013, the Burger King USA official account was hacked by pranksters who replaced Burger King imagery with the McDonald's logo and products, and stated that Burger King was being sold to McDonald's because the "Whopper flopped." The hackers continued tweeting random messages and making fun of Burger King for an hour, post which the account was suspended. McDonald's responded quickly, stating that they had nothing to do with the hack, and control of the handle was eventually restored.

McDonald's @McDonalds   23 hrs
We empathize with our @BurgerKing counterparts. Rest assured, we had nothing to do with the hacking.
Collapse   ← Reply   ↻ Retweet   ★ Favorite   ••• More

1:43 p.m. · Feb 18, 2013 · Details

3. Thou Shalt Leverage Technology

Even after implementing the second step, you may find that there are multiple people within and outside the organization who simply must have publishing access to your assets. Multiple people at the digital agency may need to publish content; multiple CRM personnel may need to issue responses; and your brand team may need to put in some final touches. In such cases, it is better to implement a publishing tool and give all personnel login access to the publishing tool and not the platform. Social Studio, HootSuite, Adobe, Sysomos, Simplify360, and many, many other tools cater to workflow management, allow customized levels of access to brand assets, and automate the workflow so that there is a recorded creator and approver for every piece of content. In organizations where legal or compliance teams check social content, an additional layer can be added for these teams that can then approve/reject content within the tool ecosystem rather than on email.

4. Thou Shalt Centralize Login Credentials

Maintain a central database of credentials that is available only to the CCO and CMO. Audit it monthly to make sure all credentials are currently valid. Run surprise checks as well. Pre-align what action will be taken if any asset credentials have been changed without updating the central database. Create a protocol where passwords are changed once a quarter and at the time of exit of any person with credentials access. No new digital assets should be published without the credentials being added to this central database. In times of emergency, this database can be accessed to delete offending material or issue statements. The credentials will also be useful to listen and respond on the company-owned assets.

5. Thy Maker ≠ Thy Checker

The person who writes tweets/post copy should never be the one approving/publishing the same copy. Institute a maker-checker process to ensure that any content published on your social assets goes through at least two sets of eyes. The maker, or copywriter, is often a creative resource, usually part of a digital agency. The checker's role is to ensure that the content being published is "on brand," free of grammatical and spelling errors, and, of course, not intended for a personal handle. Some organizations also follow a stringent legal/compliance check for every piece of social content. This slows down the process, but organizations that follow this believe that they are minimizing risks on a naturally high-risk medium.

While all this sounds complicated, it isn't all that hard to implement. Many publishing tools available today allow a maker-checker and log credentials for the maker and the checker for each individual piece of content. This ensures that everyone takes ownership of the social assets and allows for an audit in case something does go wrong.

6. Thou Shalt Not Mix Business and Pleasure

Most social media goof-ups happen when a piece of content that is intended for a personal handle ends up on an official one. Using a dedicated device for brand content builds discipline and minimizes chances of personal posts going out from a brand's handle. It also reduces the chance of there being malicious programs or vulnerabilities on the device used for brand content, protecting the account against hackers, etc.

A good example of this is KitchenAid. On October 3, 2012, the @KitchenAidUSA account tweeted, "Obamas gma even knew it was going 2 be bad! 'She died 3 days b4 he became president'. #nbcpolitics." The brand responded quickly and honestly, deleting the offending tweet and issuing an apology. Sure enough, the message had been sent in error by a member of its "Twitter team," who tweeted it from the brand's account by mistake. A dedicated device would have prevented this and saved the brand a lot of embarrassment.

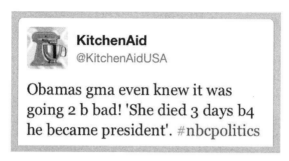

KitchenAid
@KitchenAidUSA

It was carelessly sent in error by a member of our Twitter team who, needless to say, won't be tweeting for us anymore.

← Reply ⇄ Retweet ★ Favorite ≋ Buffer

228 RETWEETS   36 FAVORITES

9:09 PM - 3 Oct 12 · Embed this Tweet

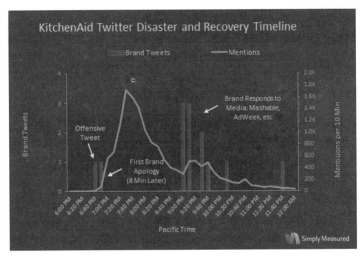

7. Thou Shalt Verify Thy Assets

It is important to ensure that all your digital assets are verified by the respective platforms they're on. Having a verified asset makes it more likely that your consumers reach out to you with questions rather than just ranting about them in general. This, in turn, means that you learn about a problem and can solve it that much faster.

It is also important to weed out all the imposters on social media who are using your brand name or visually similar names and trying to mislead people. The CCO should lead a continuous effort to identify fakes and report them to the respective platforms. Most platforms suspend such accounts or merge fake pages with official assets. Unverified pages are a ticking time bomb and can embarrass the brand or, in the worst case, set off a social crisis. Moreover, your consumers or investors are less likely to repose faith in a brand that cannot even secure its own assets.

If copyrighted content is a major source of revenue for your business, then it may also be wise to identify and appoint an agency to take down any content that violates your copyright. It's easy for individuals to steal your content and monetize it for their own benefit.

Examples

Netflix launched its service in India on January 6, 2016. Enthusiastic users started tweeting welcome messages, queries, suggestions, and complaints to the handle @netflixInd. The handle promptly responded to the tweets. Consumers and media believed @netflixInd to be the official handle (there was no verified handle for India) and were communicating with it. Forty-eight hours and one thousand tweets later, it was discovered that the handle was a fake. While the @netflixInd handle did not appear malicious, it was probably run by a cybersquatter hoping to sell the handle to Netflix at a later date. More fake handles such as @IndiaNetFlix were discovered which had started subversive activities right away, redirecting consumers to a different URL in a possible phishing attempt.

That's not the only time Netflix had Twitter trouble. On December 21, 2016, its account was hacked by a group called "OurMine" that sent out tweets mocking world security. Netflix reacted swiftly this time around, and the handle was suspended in about three hours, and the Netflix support handle acknowledged the breach immediately.

In a similar case, social comic Mike Melgaard impersonated Target customer care on Facebook (and later Doritos, Campbell's, Chobani, etc.) to make fun of trolls ranting against Target's gender-neutral kids section. It took 16 hours for Target to get it taken down, in which time many of the consumers threatened to boycott Target. While the comments were mostly amusing in this case, they left a lot of people very offended. Verified accounts help prevent cases like this; when consumers know a verified account exists, they're less likely to interact with an unverified entity.

▸ **Target** ✓
19 mins · 🌐

I shopped at Target once in while because it was convenient for me on way to work or going back home. Other stores had better prices but would still shopped at Target due to convenience . Well now that Target is trying to be overly PC and basically just want gender neutral or transgenders to shop there, I will have to go out of may way to shop elsewhere.

👍 Like   💬 Comment   ➤ Share

5 people like this.   Most Relevant ▾

◉ Write a comment...   📷

◉ **Ask ForHelp** ▮, we at Target have heard your concern.

Sorry for being nice and taking others into consideration. We know there's just too much of that going around in the world these days and it surely upsets folks like you. We'll try harder to be not as nice next time.
Like · Reply · 👍 2 · 15 mins

   ▮ Sarcasm and content is not customer service. Screen shotted this and forwarded to Corp.
   Like · 👍 1 · 12 mins

   ◉ **Ask ForHelp** ▮, please don't. I am sorry. It's my first day and this is just really frustrating dealing with all of this! 🙁 🙁
   Like · 11 mins

   ◉ Write a reply...   📷

▮ Schwartz ▸ **Target** ✓
2 mins · Riverside, CA · 🌐

And I used to love shopping at Target! Bye, bye!

Like · Comment · Share

◉ Write a comment...   📷

◉ **Ask ForHelp** Don't let the door hit yah where the good Lord split yah, ▮!
Like · Reply · 👍 1 · 1 min

   ▮ Wow, really?
   Like · Just now

   ◉ Write a reply...   📷

8. Thou Shalt Seek Out Thy Allies

Identify the right contact point in your country for the major social platforms your brand is present on. You may already be in touch with the larger platforms such as Facebook and Twitter for advertising and content, but the contact points will not be the same for reporting abuse or impersonation. Get your legal team involved; ensure that they know how to file a complaint about anything on social that could be damaging to your brand.

It is sometimes difficult to find the correct place to report a compromised asset, so we're putting the basics in here for easy reference.

For security issues on Facebook, head to https://www.facebook.com/hacked, and follow the steps to change the password and secure your handle.

For Twitter, head to https://support.twitter.com/forms, and choose the correct issue that you're facing.

For Google accounts, head to https://accounts.google.com/signin/recovery if you've been locked out of your own account.

9. Thou Shalt Safeguard Thy Customers' Data

Most businesses today store an immense amount of consumer data, including names, birthdays, email addresses, and phone numbers. In some cases, financial information such as credit card numbers, pins, and expiry dates are also stored. While proper use of this information is critical to your business's success and enhances consumer convenience, there are always hackers and malicious programs looking to steal this data from you. It's important to follow regulatory guidelines and maintain up-to-date security for consumer data. Data breaches can have far-reaching consequences.

Examples

In April 2016, bitcoin trader bitWallet was hit by a cyber-attack. While no bitcoins were actually stolen (secondary security measures prevented this), the company elected to shut down the service in May 2016.

Avid Life Media, the owner of "affairs" website ashleymadison. com, suffered a data breach in July 2015, which was more debilitating. Hackers stole 40 million consumer records, including names and postal and email addresses, and threatened to release all of these to the public if the site were not shut down. Avid refused to comply, and the hackers did end up releasing all the data, leading to multiple lawsuits and the eventual resignation of embattled CEO Noel Biderman.

Following the security protocols listed here is not always easy or convenient. Technology helps; using publishing tools and password management software can make things easier. At the end of the day though, the consequences of a mistakenly published tweet or a compromised social account are severe enough to make the additional effort worthwhile.

10. Thou Shalt Educate Thy Ambassadors

Brands often use influencers or ambassadors to post and tweet about their products on a paid basis. While the jury is still out on the ethics of this practice, it's become standard protocol for marketers, no different from asking celebrities to endorse a brand on mass media. From a crisis standpoint, it's critical to educate the celebrity (or the agency managing their digital assets) on social media etiquette. It's even more critical to reach out to them during times of crisis, asking them to pause all sponsored content until the crisis has been resolved.

Examples

On September 19, 2014, celebrity comedian Joan Rivers posted on Facebook and Instagram that she was upgrading to the iPhone 6. She spoke about how happy she'd been with the iPhone 4 she bought in 2010, and how the only issue with that old phone was the battery was giving up. The problem here was that Joan Rivers passed away on September 4, 2014, and the social content was published two weeks later. It was obviously a scheduled post, but it punched a huge hole in the Apple "we don't need endorsement" school of marketing. While the posts were deleted, social media had a field day with the screenshots.

REBSH
@Mrs_Hickling

#iPhone6 so big, Joan Rivers came back from the dead to endorse it. #JoanRivers #JoanDay #iPhone

●○○○○ T-Mobile 🛜 7:37 AM ✈ ❋ 100% 🔋 ⚡

Q Search

Joan Rivers
26 minutes ago via Instagram · 🌐

This badass is being replaced by an iPhone 6 (not the fat one). I got this one in 2010, and after 4 years, my only complaint is that apps are now designed for bigger screens, and the battery is getting tired. Never had a case for it, since it was most beautiful on its own. Great achievement in design. Great product. **#apple #iPhone #tech**

Naomi Harris
@mapledipped

Woah, @Joan_Rivers is touting the iPhone 6 on her Facebook page. Guess once a deal is in place nothing and I mean nothing can stop it.

5:50 PM - 19 Sep 2014

↩ ⟲ 2 ♥ 2

In another case, on May 19, 2016, reality star Scott Disick posted a sponsored image and caption on his Instagram account. Unfortunately, Scott forgot to delete the instructions from the brand (Bootea UK) and pasted the email including the words, "Here you go, at 4pm EST write the below: Caption—Keeping up with the summer workout routine with my morning @BooteaUK protein shake."

Once again, the posts were screenshotted before they could be deleted, and social media had fun with Scott.

In December 2015, Reliance Jio launched its 4G services in India with a big bash. It also generated a huge amount of buzz on Twitter, but for the wrong reasons. Reliance had commissioned the who's who of Bollywood to tweet in support, and sent them demo copy. Unfortunately, all the celebrities including Hrithik Roshan, John Abraham, Parineeti Chopra, and Sonakshi Sinha used the exact same copy to tweet. The tweets all read "Congratulations to the Jio family on this landmark day! This truly seems like the beginning of a Digital India. #CelebratingJio." Fans were naturally disappointed by the lack of creativity displayed by these creative artists, as well as the ability of a large corporation to control the narrative on Twitter.

In all these cases, the lapse occurred outside the organizations' control. All the principles of asset management cannot control a lapse from a third party, so education and monitoring is the best you can do in this respect.

References

Chrysler

http://www.adweek.com/adfreak/chrysler-throws-down-f-bomb-twitter-126967 (accessed on April 11, 2017).

Volkswagen

http://lighthouseinsights.in/volkswagen-india-twitter-fail-story.html/ (accessed on April 11, 2017).

Pepsi

http://timesofindia.indiatimes.com/business/india-business/Pepsi-disowns-tweet-on-Supreme-Court/articleshow/27233519.cms (accessed on April 11, 2017).

HMV

http://www.theguardian.com/business/2013/jan/31/hmv-workers-twitter-feed-sacking (accessed on April 11, 2017).

Netflix

http://www.dnaindia.com/scitech/report-fake-accounts-for-netflix-india-make-an-appearance-on-twitter-2163256 (accessed on April 11, 2017).
http://www.huffingtonpost.in/2016/01/07/netflix-india-_n_8927406.html (accessed on April 11, 2017).
http://fortune.com/2016/12/21/netflix-twitter-hack/ (accessed on April 11, 2017).

Target

https://www.buzzfeed.com/javiermoreno/a-guy-posed-as-a-target-customer-service-rep-on-facebook-to?utm_term=.iv3028ZPrL#.pxRA4eVl5X (accessed on April 11, 2017).

BitWallet

http://news.softpedia.com/news/coinwallet-bitcoin-trader-shuts-down-following-data-breach-502843.shtml (accessed on April 11, 2017).

Avid Life Media

http://krebsonsecurity.com/2015/07/online-cheating-site-ashleymadi-son-hacked/ (accessed on April 11, 2017).

Joan Rivers tweets from the dead

http://www.businessinsider.in/Oops-Joan-Rivers-Promotes-iPhone-6-
In-Pre-Scheduled-Social-Media-Posts/articleshow/42927267.cms
(accessed on April 11, 2017).

Scott Disick copy-pasted instruction on Instagram

http://mashable.com/2016/05/19/scott-disick-sponsored-
instagrams/#UtDRIu0wVmqj (accessed on April 11, 2017).

KitchenAid

http://oursocialtimes.com/kitchenaidusa-handling-a-twitter-crisis/
(accessed on April 11, 2017).
http://simplymeasured.com/blog/kitchenaid-twitter-mistake-analytics
/#sm.00019kebdjxyfeorxcr1llzzjv1i5 (accessed on April 11, 2017).

Reliance Jio

http://www.newindianexpress.com/entertainment/gossip/
CelebratingJio-Indian-Celebrities-and-Their-Cloned-Tweets-Gets-
Trolled/2015/12/28/article3200219.ece (accessed on April 11, 2017).

Chapter-5

SOCIAL MEDIA MONITORING

"Social media will help you build up loyalty of your current customers to the point that they will willingly, and for free, tell others about you."

—Bonnie Sainsbury

The incredible proliferation of social media platforms means that your stakeholders may potentially be talking about you at any time. Are you listening? Social listening and analytics is a hot topic of conversation amongst marketers and digital mavens today, and with good reason. Listening provides critical inputs for a broad range of organizational tasks and can be used by the marketing, product, and strategy teams. It can tell you how well a campaign is performing, what consumers think about your latest product, or what they feel about your competitor. You can take it a step deeper and understand what factors they evaluate while making a purchase decision or draw a demographic and geographic portrait of consumers who are interested in a particular subject.

For the purpose of this chapter, we'll restrict ourselves to only one function of social listening—brand protection.

The simplest form of listening is to track conversations around a particular tweet or campaign hashtag, understanding usage volumes and trends (day part, day of week, link to Above The Line advertising campaigns [ATL], etc.) as well as sentiment. There is a range of tools that allow marketers to do this; most of them are free (TweetDeck, Keyhole, TweetReach, etc.). It is a sound practice to use these while launching a new campaign, especially if there is a controversial element to it. Close monitoring will allow you to see if significant negativity creeps into the conversation, and to course correct or, in the worst case, pull the campaign off air!

Unfortunately, this is not nearly enough. Crises don't wait for campaigns, and they don't necessarily happen while you're watching out for them. Consumers don't use your campaign hashtags or even your brand handles when they talk about a problem with your products. They may not even choose the same platform that you do. So how do you ensure that when someone says something that could harm your brand, you get to know and take action right away?

Setting Up a Listening Practice

The great thing about social media, forums, and online news is that most platforms share data publicly through application program interfaces (APIs). A broad range of listening tools exists that can combine data from all these streams and crawl that data for mentions of your keywords. Salesforce's Radian6, Sysomos MAP, Netbase Insight Composer, Crimson Hexagon Foresight, and Brandwatch are a few tools we have personally used; there are many others available as well. While each of them have pros and cons, all of them are able to competently perform the task mentioned above—they pull in real-time or near real-time data from multiple sources and crawl that data to throw up any mentions of your keywords. A subscription to one of these tools is strongly recommended; it's pretty much a bare minimum requirement of the brand protection agenda. As your listening practice evolves, you may find the need to subscribe to more than one, but that's a call each organization needs to take for itself.

It is important to note at this stage that while listening tools pick up all data from platforms such as Twitter and Instagram, and almost all data from online news and forums, they only pick up a fraction of the data from Facebook (2%–10% of total data). This is due to Facebook's privacy policy, which only allows tools to pick up public posts. This issue is com- \ mon across tools; some may show slightly more Facebook data than others, but none of them can pick up private posts. This can be mitigated to a degree by allowing your listening tool credentials access to your brand's Facebook page. This allows the tool to pick up almost all data from your page, which enhances your ability to read Facebook, but can't really compensate for the 90% private posts. Listening tools pick up no data whatsoever from LinkedIn. This is not a huge problem at the moment, as most crises break on Facebook or Twitter, but LinkedIn is an evolving medium and it is important to keep an eye out for developments on this front.

Once you have chosen a tool, the next step is to create a brand protection query. You've already created an asset inventory and a list of sensitive areas for your organization where things can go wrong (for the crisis playbook). Now it's time to put these into a Boolean query, or a set of Boolean queries. The query starts off with your brand name, your social assets, your brand and campaign hashtags, the names of your products/product lines, anything that consumers may mention in the context of your brand.

Next, add on brand ambassadors or celebrities associated with the brand, including their personal social handles.

Remember to keep a special eye out for mentions from/about your brand ambassadors and celebrity endorsers

Finally, add the names and social handles of organization's spokespersons and other people in senior management whom consumers may mention when they talk about your brand. Add anything else that may be relevant to your category, such as flight codes for an airline, events that your brand sponsors, etc.

Once your basic query is ready, run it on the tool and have a look at the results. While word clouds or topic wheels are great, it's important to also preview a few individual statements for each major term; see what people are saying about it and what other keywords they use alongside it. A degree of cleanup will be required, removing generic terms that are throwing up results not directly related to your brand. You can also add on new terms that consumers are using in relation to your brand, which you didn't think of before.

You now have a tool that's pulling up every direct or indirect mention of your brand and allowing you to see them in real time. That's awesome, but it can also be quite overwhelming. The sheer quantum of data is so vast, it's important to remember that for now, your focus is only on brand protection.

Essentially, this means looking out for a spurt of negative mentions about some aspect of your brand. Use the sentiment filter on the tool to cull out all the negative mentions on your query. Tool-generated sentiment is only

60% accurate, but that's good enough for you to be able to identify current pain points that consumers are talking about. Create a subfilter that contains all these known negatives, and put this up on a dashboard that the listening team, CCO, and all the members of the crisis squad have access to. Your most sensitive keywords may be obvious; a restaurant chain might look out for sick or ill or poisoning or hospital or doctor or worms.

It is important to look for the not so obvious as well, for example, if a cell phone operator knows that ~90% mentions of network coverage are negative, or a carmaker knows that 80% of conversations about service are negative, they can include the words "coverage" or "service" in the negative subfilter.

Resources permitting, an analyst should monitor this dashboard at all times. For multinational organizations with consumers across the globe, a pair of analysts working in discrete locations (USA and India or Europe and Australia) can be tasked with this. The CCO should be alerted immediately about any critical issue (health, safety, criminal, financial) or any issue that crosses the crisis threshold (as determined in the crisis playbook).

Maintaining vigilance 24×7 is hard, but fortunately technology comes to the rescue again! Most of these tools have the ability to send out email alerts on specifically designated topics. The email can contain the number of mentions, the relative social influence of the authors, as well as the full text of whatever is being said. All you have to do is set up an alert for any mention of your most sensitive keywords, or above threshold mentions of any negative keyword, and the tool will send an email to a predefined set of email addresses.

These alerts can be sent via a distribution list to the entire crisis squad, or only the CCO and listening and response teams, depending on the organization's preference. You can also leverage support from your telecom operator to convert the email into a text message if needed. Once again, technology is not perfect, and you will get false alarms, but in the larger scheme of things that is infinitely preferable to there being a crisis about your brand and you not knowing about it.

The response teams should also be clued in on all the alerts, for two main reasons. A quick response to a known issue can prevent it from spiraling out of control, so a seamless workflow between listening and response is extremely desirable. If, however, the issue is truly crisis causing, the response team needs to scale up its preparedness to handle the high volume of inbound mentions that are likely to occur.

Command Centers

The last piece of the monitoring puzzle is the command center. Command centers are in vogue today; many organizations have rushed to build them without understanding how to use them or studying best practices from the industry. Simply put, a command center is a physical or virtual location where multiple sources of data (social, news, internal operations, brand website analytics, etc.) are displayed in an easily comprehensible form on a series of live dashboards. While command centers can be extremely useful, there are a few principles to follow before building one to ensure you get maximum bang for your buck.

Assign a primary purpose to the command center. What is the one really important thing you want it to achieve? Brand protection? Consumer insight? Campaign metrics? Identify what you're going to do with the data and insights before you build out. You can, of course, recalibrate once it's up and running, but it's important to go in with a clear purpose.

Integrate multiple datasets, especially internal product data. Reading social data alone is important for marketing, but the ability to read spikes in social mentions in conjunction with online sales of a new product, or flight operations data, or news about a change in government policy gives the command center real meaning.

Democratize data—The command center should not be a closed room where only analysts can enter. The idea is to make information available to relevant stakeholders wherever they are and to allow all those working on a brand to know what their consumers

are saying. To begin with, the room itself (if there is one) should be an inviting room with glass walls so that anyone can have a look inside. You can even conduct tours for employees, so that everyone knows what's going on. Mobile dashboards are useful as well, so people can access crucial information about their piece of the business, no matter where they are located. Finally, putting up physical screens in high traffic parts of the office or outside senior management cabins is a good way to make sure employees are in sync with the voice of the consumer.

Chapter-6

STORYCRAFTING

*"Marketing is no longer
about the stuff you make,
but about the stories you tell."*

—Seth Godin

The early days of a crisis tend to generate a huge amount of information, opinions, and stories. It's important to create a story of your own and carry the narrative through until the end of the crisis. Storycrafting is the most important communications aspect of crisis management. First up, you need to keep in mind the different cohorts that consumers are likely to split into at this stage. To make this more relatable, we have employed the example of the Volkswagen #dieselgate emissions scandal.

Your brand loyalists, who will defend you (up to a point), mostly because of their own investment in the brand. They may be long-time consumers and may have recommended your brand to friends and family. For them, it's a personal admission that they were wrong, and they're unwilling to make that admission without damning evidence against you. Sharing your story with this group gives them an incentive to remain loyal for longer and arms them with a counter point of view that they can quote from on public platforms.

When the Volkswagen scandal broke, there were shocked reactions from loyalists. In the medium term, however, messages of support converged around three major stories.

\# The fact that the organization had come forward on its own, with full disclosure and responsibility, and had apologized without reservation. While this was not entirely true, because Volkswagen would have had to reveal the facts in a few months in any case, it's a strong story that it was able to sell to its loyalists. Consumers began tweeting things like "I gotta hand it to them for owning the problem rather than making excuses."

\# The story that it was committed to making things right. It fired its CEO and set aside an astronomical sum of money to do this. It was also working proactively with government agencies in countries where it didn't have to. (Volkswagen subsequently recalled 800,000

cars in India to fix the problem, even though it wasn't required to do so by law.)

\# Some loyalists also came out to state that they hadn't bought a VW for economy anyways and were happy with the safety, reliability, and performance of the car. We do not know if this was a story Volkswagen chose to disseminate, but it certainly helped.

philinhongkong
@philinhongkong

Im pretty sure I didn't buy a golf GTi based on its carbon footprint #Volkswagen

RETWEETS LIKES
2   4

6:53 PM - 22 Sep 2015

\# The low-involvement consumers, who will stay on the sidelines. These consumers are unlikely to commit to either side of the debate but may temporarily switch to a different brand or avoid the category altogether until the issue has been settled. This group is willing to hear your side of the story but will see the absence of a statement as an admission of guilt or an expression of arrogance. Individualized responses with linked material (articles, photos, videos) reassure them that the brand cares deeply about its customers and is taking their concerns seriously. They can also be invited for facility visits or other "proofs of process" to rebuild their faith in the brand. It's important to engage this group with facts and concrete actions so they remain interested in the narrative and withhold judgment until the end.

In Volkswagen's case, the jury's still out on this one. Replacement cycles in the automobile industry are very long, and it remains to be seen if consumers will go back to the brand. Neutrals tweeted things like "@ BBC_Haveyoursay though very disappointed. This is my first VW. May just turn out to be my last. The situation is just criminal." The fact that the brand is still in the consideration set, when many commentators suggested that the scandal would lead to bankruptcy, indicates that it's holding on.

Milhir
@MilhirBajoria   ⚲ Follow

Replying to @BBC_HaveYourSay

@BBC_HaveYourSay though very disappointed. This is my first VW. May just turn out to be my last. The situation is just criminal #volkswagen

6:47 PM · 22 Sep 2015 from Kensington, London

Your detractors, either consumers who've had a bad experience with the brand and nurse a grudge or those who consume a competitive brand and are convinced of its superiority. They will be the first to denounce you on social media and will try and drum up support to ban your product or otherwise impact your business, as this plays back to their conviction that they picked the winner and were right in never trusting you. This group is unlikely to be open to debate and will keep firing the same arsenal back at you on social media. Engaging this set in public one-to-one conversation is a bad idea; share a statement and welcome them into an offline conversation, where you can attempt a resolution.

When it came to Volkswagen, it wasn't just dealing with supporters of competitive brands, but those of a competitive technology. Petrol-heads have long maintained that diesel is an inferior technology. They tweeted things like "In light of #dieselgate I'm more convinced than ever that a 6-litre V12 is the way forward." Environmentalists have long stated that diesel is polluting, a key cause of deteriorating air quality, and should not be used for passenger vehicles. They tweeted things like "Talk dirty to me," she begged. "Alright," he said, leaning closer, "Volkswagen Diesel."

There's little headway that Volkswagen could make with these consumers at the best of times, and almost none during this crisis. Volkswagen wisely stuck to making regular public announcements, sharing progress on recalls and avoiding confrontation.

Having understood the needs of these consumers, we can arrive at a few critical elements to storycrafting.

Timing

Get your first response out quickly, ideally on the same day the crisis breaks. The story can be delivered in stages, starting with "We know about it" to moving to "We've identified the problem" and then on to "this is what we're doing to fix it." The final communication should tell consumers that the issue has been completely resolved (or resolved to the extent possible). This gives your loyalists the signal to start recommending your brand again and tells the flirts that your brand can now be allowed to reenter their consideration set.

In July 2013, a Southwest Airlines plane landed belly up at New York's La Guardia Airport. The company quickly posted a holding statement on its social handles, followed by a detailed response mentioning that an emergency evacuation was underway. Eight people were injured in the incident, which was later ruled to be the pilot's fault. Southwest went on to terminate the pilot.

The important thing here is that Southwest immediately acknowledged the situation and willingly shared transparent updates with its consumers and went on to take concrete action against an erring employee. These actions saved it from a larger PR crisis.

Southwest Airlines
July 22

Southwest Airlines confirms emergency responders at New York's LaGuardia airport are assisting with an evacuation of #flight345 after the Boeing 737 arrived this evening from Nashville. We will provide further details when available.

Like · Comment · Share   1,151

👍 4,987 people like this.   Top Comments ▾

| Write a comment... |

⟨ I love that Southwest actually comes out and tells us first without waiting for pressure from the media.
Like · Reply · 👍 449 · July 22 at 6:33pm via mobile

💬 5 Replies

y I was on the flight and would like to say that so far we are all okay! Thanks for the prayers!
Like · Reply · 👍 725 · July 22 at 6:34pm via mobile

💬 32 Replies

💬 View more comments   2 of 652

The Storyteller

Choose the correct spokesperson for each audience. The CEO is a great option to speak to consumers, either directly or via the news media. They like to see that the company is taking the problem seriously, with direct involvement at the highest level. Your CEO may not be the best equipped to solve a manufacturing crisis, but he/she needs to be there and he/she needs to be visible.

The COO and CFO are appropriate spokespersons for briefing analysts and shareholders; they have the right credentials to speak on the business impact of the crisis, how long it will take for the brand to regain its position in the category, etc. Shareholders are also more likely to trust them to minimize the financial impact of the crisis, as the financial performance of the company is their direct responsibility.

Content

If your organization has in any way led to the crisis, apologize immediately, sincerely, and without reservation. Focus on the impact on consumers and the lay public, assure them that the organization is leaving no stone unturned to fix whatever went wrong. Get the text of the apology read by a panel of consumers/neutral third parties to ensure that it tells the right story. Assume that pieces will be quoted out of context, remove anything inflammatory. Don't make it about you, or even your employees, partners, or shareholders. This is especially important if the crisis stretches over weeks or months, as the temptation to self-pity is much higher.

After you've accepted responsibility, switch to constructive, concrete updates. Show evidence (photos, videos, independent news reports) of action being taken on the ground. Share an honest assessment of the total damage done, as well as achievable timelines by when things will be fixed.

Remember that body language and behavior are just as important as the content itself. The storyteller's body language should be sincerely apologetic; trying to ease the situation with self-deprecating humor does not work. At the same time he/she should not appear to have given up but should be driven by the need to fix the problem. The company's top management, especially the spokespersons, will be under the media scanner for the duration of the crisis. Avoid ostentatious purchases or attendance at public parties or social events during this time. Also avoid any behavior that can be construed as illegal, unethical, or immoral at a personal or professional level.

Multinational corporations also need to be careful about local relevance if the crisis has occurred outside the organization's home country. Phrases and gestures can mean different things across different cultures, and it's usually better to identify a senior local executive who can accompany the CEO. If such a person is not identifiable, hire an outsider to spearhead the cleanup, keeping in mind his/her past track record and local appeal. In the BP case, Tony Hayward's "Britishness" rubbed Americans the wrong way, leading to even poorer results from his PR efforts.

Platform and Packaging

The first response to a crisis should ideally be on the same platform where it originates, in an attempt to contain it to that platform. The next step, of course, is to open it up to mainstream news media after which the platform becomes less relevant.

Subsequent communication should be multiplatform, once again prioritizing speed and efficiency over style and stature. Consumers are more likely to resonate with a mobile phone-shot video from the CEO at the location with his/her sleeves rolled up than an expensive, slickly produced commercial backed by an expensive media plan. YouTube, Facebook, and Twitter (Periscope) all offer live video options, which can be targeted and promoted to maximize relevant reach.

Social Brand Voice

Brands are built on the back of personality, and the way you articulate that personality on your social handles is what we call "brand voice." Brand voice is the glue that connects the brand lovers with the brand. A loyal fan base in turn can become the front line of defense in times of crises.

We have mentioned before that humor is generally avoidable. There are rare occasions on which it works, but these are usually minor, victimless crises. For example, an employee of the American Red Cross once tweeted, "Ryan found two more

4 bottle packs of Dogfish Head's Midas Touch beer ... when we drink we do it right #gettngslizzerd." The organization deleted the tweet soon after and followed it up with "We've deleted the rogue tweet, but rest assured the Red Cross is sober and we have confiscated the keys." Here, the Red Cross combined two things we don't usually recommend, deleting a tweet and joking about it. The harmless nature of the error and the creativity of the response took the sting out of what could have snowballed into a larger issue.

Creativity inspires people. Communication that smartly leverages creativity can strike a chord with consumers and media and help douse a crisis. After all, if creative ideas can build brands, then why underestimate the power of creativity when it comes to brand protection?

In August 2014, popular UK bakery chain Greggs found that an insulting version of their logo with the tagline "Providing shit to scum for 70 years" was showing up on Google image search and had led to a trend on Twitter. Its Wikipedia page had also been vandalized to show the incorrect logo. Greggs immediately acknowledged the issue on social, and instead of stating the obvious "We're working with Google to take it down," it tweeted a photo of a tray of donuts, offering them to Google UK as a reward if they were able to #FixGreggs. Not to be left behind, Google UK replied saying, "Throw in a sausage roll and we'll get it fixed ASAP."

Some hours later, the offending logo had disappeared. Greggs took it a step further by tweeting a picture of the Google logo spelt with their sausage rolls and said "Maybe those kind folks @GoogleUK could give us the doodle tomorrow."

Once again, since this was a relatively victimless crisis, and both Greggs and Google had humor as an intrinsic part of their brand voice, they were able to get creative with their crisis comms and build their respective brands while they resolved the issue.

Replying to @GreggsOfficial

Sorry @GreggstheBakers, we're on it. Throw in a sausage roll and we'll get it done ASAP. #fixgreggs

RETWEETS 466 LIKES 297

Censorship

We've discussed the things a brand can do to ensure that its side of the story gets heard. It's important, however, to allow others to tell their story as well. Don't delete negative comments from your social pages; don't block people who're asking hard questions. Of course, if you have existing policies to delete and ban commenters for profanity, you can continue with that practice.

Social media is viral by nature; any attempt to throttle news only encourages a more rapid spread. Acknowledging the issue and responding with both action and communication is the correct approach in today's information-overloaded environment.

Special Note: Issuing a Denial

Speed is especially critical if you're sure that the organization is being falsely accused and intend to deny that a problem has occurred. If you wait more than 24 hours to issue a denial, it will start to seem like a cover-up. Give clear evidence in your favor. Videos and images are more believable than just a statement, so CCTV or equivalent footage is an asset. Back up your assessment with statements from credible outsiders, preferably government agencies, as soon as possible. For example, in the Lipton Green Tea fake worms case (details in Chapter 1), the brand got the food assessment authority of the municipality of Dubai to put out a statement defending the product and condemning the rumors.

Matters get more complicated if you're unsure whether your organization is at fault or not. On July 30, 2013, the US states of Iowa, Nebraska, and Texas declared an outbreak of cases of cyclospora. The authorities in Iowa and Nebraska identified a link to salads eaten at the Red Lobster and Olive Garden restaurants owned by Darden Restaurants. They further traced the source of the parasite to fresh greens used in the salads, which had been procured from Taylor Farms de Mexico. The Center for Disease Control and Prevention (CDC) and FDA sent a team to Mexico to investigate. At this time, Taylor Farms had no way of knowing whether it was guilty and no way to prove that it was innocent. It responded by taking preemptive action—on August 12, it voluntarily recalled all potentially contaminated produce from the market and shut down production. It further committed that it would not restart production until cleared by the FDA team.

The FDA team conducted an environmental analysis and found no traces of cyclospora on site. They also determined that operations conducted by Taylor Farms were in accordance with food safety norms, post which Taylor recommenced production. The rapid proactive steps and announcements made by Taylor management minimized the negative PR and allowed it to resume business quickly after the facility was cleared. Had Nestle India followed the same protocol with Maggi—a voluntary withdrawal and production halt pending regulatory approval—it would probably have been able to bounce back quicker. The only criticism of Taylor's crisis management efforts is perhaps that it did not finish the story and provide consumers with closure. It should have communicated the results of the FDA assessment and ensured that consumers and the media knew that it'd been given a clean chit. Many articles about the issue still hold Taylor responsible and have not been updated since early August 2013. Good social listening would have enabled it to identify these publications and ask for a correction/ redaction.

At the end of the day, consumers realize that an organization is just as prone to error as a human being. As long as you respond to their concerns in a timely, honest, and constructive manner, the damage can be contained. Always place the interests of your consumers above that of your internal stakeholders and use humor with extreme caution when spinning your organization's crisis response story.

References

Volkswagen Diesel

http://www.visibrain.com/en/blog/volkswagen-dieselgate-crisis-twitter-analysis/ (accessed on April 11, 2017).
http://www.bbc.com/news/business-34322961 (accessed on April 11, 2017).

Taylor Farms de Mexico

http://www.foodsafetymagazine.com/magazine-archive1/augustsep-tember-2015/outbreak-responders-work-to-stop-viral-and-parasitic-foodborne-outbreaks/ (accessed on April 11, 2017).

Southwest Airlines

http://blog.spinweb.net/3-great-examples-of-crisis-management-on-social-media (accessed on April 11, 2017).

Greggs Bakery Case

http://www.mycustomer.com/experience/voice-of-the-customer/social-listening-and-crisis-management-how-social-can-save-your (accessed on April 11, 2017).
http://www.inquisitr.com/1424498/greggs-bakery-logo-gets-bombed-by-google/ (accessed on April 11, 2017).

Chapter-7

EXECUTION

> "Don't say anything online
> that you wouldn't want
> plastered on a billboard with
> your face on it."
>
> —Erin Bury

You've set up a crisis squad, your early warning system is in place, and you've got a great playbook for managing any crisis that may arise. So what's the point of this chapter? All you have to do is follow the playbook, right? Right, but it's rarely that simple. There will always be unexpected aspects to any crisis situation, ones that you can't predict. There may be disorienting levels of abuse from consumers or unnecessary personal attacks on leadership. There may be local politicians who choose to make a crisis into a voter issue and threaten disproportionate punishment. The ability to keep a cool head and unflinchingly execute the crisis playbook at this time will be what makes or mars your organization's crisis response.

The idea behind this chapter is to highlight some behaviors that you should or shouldn't exhibit during a crisis. We've also included a few suggestions that you can put in place during the execution phase, that allow you to come back strongly once the crisis has been resolved.

Do's

☑ Be prepared. Fire departments always stay on high alert. Even when there has been no fire reported for months, they have a rigorous training/mock drill schedule that makes them prepared for any eventuality. That is the kind of rigor the crisis team needs to have. Run a quarterly meeting of the crisis squad even if there is no crisis. Simulate through mock drills and role-plays. Keep everyone on their toes.

☑ When the crisis hits, members of the squad may be away on holiday or traveling for business. Everyone should have the updated playbook with them—soft or hard copy. It can be hosted on a web destination, but remember to maintain physical copies as well in case of a server breakdown or internet access issues.

☑ Focus on outcome, not on articulation. It's important to craft the perfect story, but it's more important that the story has the right impact on your consumers at the right time. It's easy to overintellectualize this and become indecisive, so it's critical to focus on the end goal and solve for that.

☑ When in doubt, respond disproportionately in favor of the consumer. If there's a product issue, shut the factory, facility, or restaurant where the issue originated. If products are in the supply chain or marketplace, cast a wide recall net that includes every possibly contaminated or malfunctioning product. Don't let bad news trickle out, leading to multiple admissions and apologies.

In 2015, a listeria outbreak in Arizona, Kansas, Oklahoma, and Texas was traced to the Blue Bell ice cream company, leading to a company-wide shutdown. The company had known about the listeria problem for at least four months before that and had started retrieving specific products on February 13, 2015, without making any public announcements about a health risk. On March 10, Blue Bell shut down a production line at its flagship Brenham plant, and on March 13, the brand announced a recall, calling it the first in 108 years. The company's spokesperson informed consumers that it had "voluntarily" recalled specific products due to a "potential" listeria risk, and that there was absolutely no risk in consuming any of its other products. On March 22 and April 3, the company announced further recalls and the temporary closure of its Oklahoma plant. By this time, it'd shut two of its four plants, but the worst was yet to come. On April 22, listeria was found in a fresh set of Blue Bell products, and the company finally had to recall all of its products and suspend manufacturing across all its plants. Even at this stage, the company underestimated the seriousness of the issue and promised to clean up and return within a few weeks. It took months, during which 1,400 of its employees were laid off and another 1,400 were furloughed. The brand eventually relaunched in August, but in 15 states versus the original 23. The strong heritage of the brand and the large number of loyalists will probably ensure survival, but the company escaped bankruptcy only due to a loan commitment of US$125 million from an outside investor.

In retrospect, it seems obvious that Blue Bell should have identified the root cause of the problem and executed a complete shutdown and recall in January 2015. At the time, though, they were trying to preserve market share and keep products in stores while dealing with issues one by one. In cases like this, it's important to execute a disproportionate response and place consumers' interests ahead of all other stakeholders.

A little overkill is far better than recall drip, with successive bouts of damage to the brand reputation, employee morale, and long-term sales.

☑ Designate a "war room" and block it for the duration of the crisis. If your organization has invested in a command center, then that's the natural choice. If not, then any room will do. Pull in critical equipment, such as videoconferencing and printers/shredders. The CCO should work out of this room until the crisis is over. Ideally, pick a room where you can shoot basic AVs or video statements; all you need is good lighting, low ambient noise, and a plain wall in the background.

☑ Meet daily. Block a 10-minute meeting slot at the start of business hours every day. Attendance should be mandatory for the members of the crisis squad, who can pull in anyone else who needs to be there. This will ensure the whole squad is up to date on whatever is going on, and that the crisis remains everyone's top priority until it is resolved.

☑ Update regularly. Set up an automated or analyst-driven mechanism to send updates to all stakeholders about the situation on social, digital, and the news every two hours. Timely updates give a sense of control, as well as rescue the CCO and his/her team from constant questions about what consumers are saying about the crisis.

☑ Set up crisis comms. Create a dedicated channel of communication for the crisis squad, such as a WhatsApp or IM group, that can be accessed on mobile. This is especially critical in cases where your company's IT system has been compromised, which is what happened to Sony when its servers were penetrated by suspected North Korean hackers. The company lost access to its email server, so employees could not communicate with each other via official email. They switched to SMS and face-to-face meetings and rode out the crisis. Delete or deactivate the group after the crisis has ended to prevent it from becoming a destination for idle chatter, leading to a blind spot.

☑ Declare the crisis resolved and the issue closed. Once the immediate tasks have been completed, and business is back to normal, it's important to formally call time of closure. It's a positive signal for partners and employees that the problem has been solved, and they can resume delivering their piece of the business with complete confidence. It's also a signal to consumers that they can resume purchasing your products/services, before a full-blown campaign hits the airwaves.

Don'ts

☒ Don't forego attention to detail. Everyone will be under immense pressure during a crisis, so it's important to maintain hygiene checks on any piece of content that the brand issues. Wherever possible, run communication through a panel of consumers to make sure they're interpreting the story the way you intended.

☒ Don't try to follow the playbook by letter or sequence. Be dynamic, respond to the situation at hand and apply the appropriate part of the playbook. If you feel that an aspect of your story is being well received, then play it up. If consumers are finding it hard to comprehend or relate to something your brand has said, then simplify it through FAQs on a web destination. If they're reacting negatively to the story as a whole, then go back to the drawing board and recraft it.

☒ Don't rush to contain the crisis without fully understanding the root cause. Yes, timely communication is critical, but the objective should be to assure consumers that you're doing everything you can to solve the problem, not shush them or save face. It's OK to admit that you don't know everything right from the start; take consumers through your process of discovery and resolution.

A classic example of this is the mercury pollution in Kodaikanal, India, caused by a thermometer factory built by Pond's and eventually owned by Unilever after it bought Chesebrough-Pond's in 1987. The factory was moved to India from the USA due to increasing awareness of the hazards related to working with mercury. It was set up in an eco-sensitive area, and the workers were not taught about the risks or issued with protective gear. Factory runoff was allowed to pollute local water bodies. Unilever, to its credit, shut the factory down in 2001. It issued a statement that 5 tonnes of glass waste containing 0.15% residual mercury had been sold to a local scrap dealer, in contravention of the company's norms. However, the company dismissed claims of any health impact of the factory on employees or local residents and no effect on the environment.

In spite of strong evidence that this stance was wrong, Unilever continued to maintain it until July 2015, when a video made by Chennai rapper Sofia Ashraf went viral on YouTube, racking up 4 million views. A parallel online petition was signed 100,000 times, and the video was featured on international news platforms including *The New York Times* and *The Huffington Post*. Unilever went into crisis mode, issuing statements, putting up an FAQ section on its website, proposing cleanup norms, and working with local government to monitor the environment in the area. In 2016, Unilever arrived at a financial settlement of an undisclosed amount with 600 former employees. However, the mercury levels in the surrounding area are still at 12-25 times the defined norms in the USA or UK, and the organization continues to receive bad press.

Unilever's statements on the issue appear to have been aimed at keeping the issue under wraps and limiting the impact of what it perceived as a problem not of its making. The organization should have identified the root cause in 2001 and taken appropriate action at the time, rather than responding to social media pressure 15 years later. Even now, Unilever seems more interested in settlement and closure, rather than an enduring environmentally friendly solution, and this issue will continue to impact what is now a massive, critical market for the organization.

- ☒ Don't panic when faced with circumstances outside of the playbook. This is a crisis; unforeseen stuff will happen! Follow the principles of crisis response—be timely, honest, and constructive. It's important to be truthful and logical with consumers; they can easily see through bluster.

☒ Don't be afraid to call on anyone in the company at any time of day or night. If it's a real crisis, they'll understand. Even if they refuse or are unable to help, they may direct you to a person who can.

☒ Don't forget to plan for business resumption, even while the crisis is on. This is hard, because at its peak a crisis may consume all of your time and mental bandwidth. It's important to think beyond, plan when to restart production, and align distribution partners and sales channels to be ready to resume selling the product. Modern supply chains often build in a lot of lead time, and it may take months after the crisis is resolved to regain full supply and sales volumes. Strong brands can usually regain their leadership positions, but every month that they don't is a lost opportunity.

☒ Don't try to sidestep the crisis by sales incentives or discounts to consumers until the crisis has been decisively resolved. They need to know that you're investing all your efforts in fixing the problem, not sidestepping it.

☒ Don't threaten legal or other punitive action if you don't mean to follow through on it. It's tempting to threaten to sue for slander, but it's a lot harder to prove it in court. Once the business environment knows you won't follow through, your ability to use legal recourse as a deterrent will be severely hampered.

References

Blue Bell Ice Cream

http://fortune.com/2015/09/25/blue-bell-listeria-recall/ (accessed on April 11, 2017).

Sony Pictures Hack

https://hbr.org/2015/07/they-burned-the-house-down (accessed on April 11, 2017).

Unilever Kodaikanal

http://www.business-standard.com/article/companies/hul-settles-dispute-with-kodaikanal-unit-staff-116030900445_1.html (accessed on April 11, 2017).

http://www.newindianexpress.com/cities/chennai/Mercury-levels-still-soaring-in-Kodai/2016/06/16/article3484548.ece (accessed on April 11, 2017).

http://www.newindianexpress.com/states/tamil_nadu/15-Years-on-Unilever-Pays-Workers-Affected-by-Mercury-Poisoning-in-Kodai-kanal/2016/03/09/article3318269.ece (accessed on April 11, 2017).

Chapter-8

AFTER THE STORM

> "If you make customers unhappy in
> the physical world, they might each tell 6 friends.
> If you make customers unhappy on the Internet,
> they can each tell 6000 friends."
>
> —Jeff Bezos

Once the crisis has been resolved, and business is getting back to its normal pace, it's natural to relax. There's nothing wrong with taking it easy for a day or two; but once back, it's important to create a record of the crisis and the organization's response to it, which can be appended to the crisis playbook. This will refine the organization's crisis-handling capability and ensure that the next crisis is better managed!

It's crucial to be completely objective and answer the difficult questions with complete honesty. If you have engaged an external party to help resolve the crisis, they can also help by adding an outsider's point of view to the record.

We've included 10 key points that should be logged, but you can add others if needed.

1. Inception

Was the organization able to identify the real root cause of the problem?

#gettotherootoftheproblem

If the root cause has been identified, make sure that it cannot recur. If not, or if there is any vestige of doubt, you're looking at a situation where a crisis may recur after a few months or years. Some issues are endemic to an industry or technology and can never be completely eliminated.

The quick service restaurants (QSR) industry, for example, has seen repetitive crises driven either by contamination of ingredients (Chipotle, Olive Garden) or by employee malpractice (Domino's, KFC Australia). If this is the case, maximize scrutiny and penalties and focus organizational energy on tracking to contain problems before they become full-blown crises.

Also identify the consumer or influencer who started the fire. If this person was genuinely impacted by the brand, go out of your way to ensure that he/she has a wonderful experience henceforth. If, however, you suspect ulterior motives or malintent, place a permanent tracker on his/her social activities and prepare an individual specific response for him/her.

In the DKNY Bangkok case (referenced in Chapter 3), the influencer was Brandon Stanton, the owner of the Humans of New York Facebook page. He was genuinely wronged, and DKNY did well to ensure that his charity of choice was compensated.

2. Ownership

#OwnIt

Identify the function or facility that was originally impacted, leading to the crisis. Was there an error or lapse that caused the crisis? Was it person- or process-driven? If there were no mistakes, is there a loophole in the standard operating procedure (SOP) or are safety guidelines inadequate? Be very reticent to attribute the crisis solely to external factors and dismiss it as a one-off.

3. Social Listening and CRM

#PickingUpTheCrisis

Did your social listening and CRM practice pick up the crisis early enough? If yes, then were they escalated quickly enough, and was the CCO able to use social intelligence to limit the extent of the crisis? If not, then why? Was there a gap in the alert setup? Was it a person or tool failure? Did senior organizational stakeholders ignore the warnings? It may be wise to take corrective action depending on the circumstances behind the lapse.

The second important piece to evaluate is the spread of the crisis on social media over time. Were there inflexion points, and what caused them? They are likely to be influencer-driven. Identify the influencers who spoke for and against your brand and add them to the list in your crisis playbook. If a particular company statement or action caused an inflexion point, then scrutinize it. What unspoken rule did you break to get consumers to break their silence? What was the emotion behind that outburst?

On November 13, 2015, Sachin Tendulkar had a series of bad experiences with British Airways (BA). He tweeted out in frustration when it lost his bags. The CRM team at BA responded with a template tweet, asking him his full name, address, and baggage reference number. Given the following that Sachin has around the world, this was a mistake. BA's timeline was flooded with barbs, threats, and a whole lot of jokes, including suggestions that Sachin send them the scorecard from the 2008 Chennai test match to let them know who he was. The handle actually went down for a few minutes due to the rate at which it was bombarded. Now from BA's perspective, it didn't do much wrong. It followed the CRM process and asked for more information.

However, in the eyes of millions of Sachin's fans, it had broken the unwritten rule of treating Sachin as "God." Of course, the airline apologized in due time, fixed the problem, and Sachin followed up with a tweet stating that all was well and thanks very much for all the fan support.

4. The Crisis Squad

#TheCrisisSquad

Did the team pull together to solve the problem? Was everyone clear about their roles? Was there conflict, and, if yes, was it constructive? If a skillset was missing, add it. If a person outside the squad contributed immensely, recruit them to the squad. If any member of the team was unable to perform their role, consider a replacement.

5. The Playbook

#ThePlaybookEvaluation

Was the playbook an adequate guide through the crisis? While there may be a couple of things that you didn't plan for, the playbook should cover at least 80% of the tasks that needed to be accomplished during the crisis. If not, then a reevaluation is in order. In any case, there will be minor updates to be made to incorporate the valuable insight gained from going through an actual crisis.

Recognize and Reward

During the crisis, you will make great demands on people's time and effort. There will be late nights, weekends, and a lot of stress and sacrifices. After it's all over, it's a good practice to recognize the people who contributed to making the crisis go away.

At the very least, send out a personalized thank you email acknowledging their efforts. If you can go a step further, organize a lunch for the entire team (nothing over the top, just a chance to regroup) and recognize individuals who went above and beyond the call of duty. It's important that this is led by the CCO or CMO.

Recognizing individuals is a good way to ensure that they'll put in the same level of effort the next time a crisis calls. The stakeholders who do not get recognized may also be motivated to contribute more the next time around, so that they get their share of recognition. You cannot overestimate the value of a good team when handling a crisis, so it's important to keep them all positive, driven, and ready to roll.

Also evaluate the third parties (labs, content creators, influencers) you were able to leverage in handling the crisis. Did they deliver on set terms and turnaround times? Were the video responses executed well, with minimum fuss? Did your influencers help stem the flow and turn things around for you? If yes, then recognize them as well. If no, then evaluate replacements.

6. Execution

#HowEffectiveWasIt?

Did the response execution kick off quickly enough? Did you issue the first response within two hours? Was there a sudden overriding senior management directive to "wait and watch"? Was the team able to respond as planned? Were there departures from the process defined in the playbook, and, if so, then why? There's always a temptation to forget everything and do what seems right in the moment, but the entire point of having a crisis plan is that you don't have to think under pressure.

7. Storytelling

#IsYourStoryGoodEnough?

Was the organization's story good enough? How does one evaluate this? For starters, were you able to contain the crisis—did the volume or sentiment of crisis mentions improve after the story was launched? Did it equip your loyalists and enable them to mount a defense? On the flip side, did the story impact you negatively? Did it lead to more negativity around the brand? Was it subjected to disbelief, or did the brand come off sounding arrogant or disinterested?

In February 2013, a pastor dining at Applebee's questioned the 18% tip included in her bill and reduced it to 10% with the comment "I give God 10%, why do you get 18?" A waitress at the restaurant (who incidentally did not serve the pastor) took a picture of the receipt and posted it online. The pastor found out about the picture and asked the restaurant management how such a thing was possible. Sensing a problem, the restaurant identified the employee responsible and terminated her for breaching the organization's social media policy by posting internal information online without prior permission. It then proactively posted on its Facebook wall, stating

> We wish this situation hadn't happened. Our Guests' personal information—including their meal check—is private, and neither Applebee's nor its franchisees have a right to share this information publicly. We value our Guests' trust above all else. Our franchisee has apologized to the Guest and has taken disciplinary action with the Team Member for violating their Guest's right to privacy.

Tipping is a sensitive subject in the USA, and in this case the mob went with the waitress. They stormed Applebee's Facebook page with the usual boycott threats, asking it to take back the waitress and stand up for its employees. While the organization wanted it to be a story about managing consumer information, and breach of the organization's privacy policy, it became a class discussion about minimum wage and how wait-staff live off tips. Applebee's tried to answer every comment, and when it realized it couldn't, it hid its own post, taking all the comments with it. Consumers immediately began to slam it for censorship, when what it was really guilty of was being digitally un-savvy and unprepared for crises.

While Applebee's was prompt, proactive, and had put its consumers first, it did not think through the ramifications of the story it tried to create. Had it copy-tested the message with lay consumers, it might have been able to edit it to focus on the point it wanted to come across, that it wasn't about how much anyone should tip but about the sanctity of private information.

Evaluating a story is a qualitative and subjective process, and once again you may choose to use an external partner to do an unbiased job of it (obviously not the same external partner who helped craft it).

8. Challenges

#FeelingTroubled?

What were the key challenges faced? Were they internal? For example, did you face difficulties in accessing senior leadership, or did legal approvals take longer than expected? Was there an individual or a function that impeded the crisis management process either by dismissing the importance of consumer communication or by being defensive about their domain?

What was the key external challenge? Did a local government or regulatory body take unexpected steps leading to a forced change in the crisis plan? Did competitors enter the fray to take potshots at your brand? Was there an organized activity by an NGO or interest group?

9. Brand Impact

#CorrectiveAction

In the playbook section, we'd advised kicking off brand trackers immediately to gauge the impact of the crisis on key metrics such as brand affinity and intent to purchase. It's now time to study the movement on those metrics and decide what level of corrective action needs to be taken. It may be appropriate to hire a celebrity to place his/her personal equity alongside that of the brand and start the recovery. Cadbury did this successfully with Amitabh Bachchan (Chapter 1).

If the impact on the brand is limited, but the impact on sales is more severe (Maggi India case from Chapter 1), focus on getting supply back into the market ASAP and leverage discounts or sales incentives to aggressively regain market share.

10. Financial Impact

#HowBadWasTheBlow?

What was the impact on financials—revenue, market share, profitability? Again, it's important to be objective here; don't attempt to underplay the effects of the crisis. Convey this to stakeholders early, along with a clear road to recovery. Employ a third-party auditor if there is any ambiguity. Don't give analysts too much time or opportunity to speculate about this.

In the social age that we live in, it's very easy to get into a crisis. Consumers and comedians can be irreverent, rude, sexist, or racist, but brands need to be politically correct while still being cool. Every aspect of every business can come under public scrutiny at any time, and everyone with a smartphone and a social account becomes an instant investigative journalist. For retail organizations with thousands of consumer-facing touch-points and employees, this becomes a particularly important challenge.

We'll end this book as we started it, by reminding you that crisis is almost inevitable. Crisis readiness is no longer a choice, it's a necessity. For a crisis-ready organization, however, a crisis is just one of the threats in the business environment to be planned for and managed like any other. There is a method to the madness. And we hope that this book has given you some insights and practical hands-on advice on how to plan for and deal with crisis situations in the social age. For brands that offer a strong promise, and deliver it with clear personality and voice, no crisis is insurmountable. Such brands will remain indestructible!

#PrepareForTheWorst

#HopeForTheBest

References

British Airways Sachin Tendulkar

http://www.firstpost.com/sports/british-airways-doesnt-know-sachins-full-name-twitter-reacts-after-airline-makes-tendulkar-angry-2504984.html (accessed on April 11, 2017).

Applebee's

http://www.nbcnews.com/business/applebees-social-media-faux-pas-learning-experience-1B8251556 (accessed on April 11, 2017).